MOUNTAIN BIKE G

D0192343

Western NC Pisgah

almond, nc

VOLUME II · BY JIM PARHAM

Copyright ©1992, 1995 & 2002 by Jim Parham
3rd Revised edition 1st printing May 2002

Milestone Press, Inc., P.O. Box 158, Almond, NC 28702
www.milestonepress.com

Book design by Ron Roman/Treehouse Communications
www.treehousecomm.com

Library of Congress Cataloging-in-Publication Data

Parham, Jim.
        Off the beaten track / Jim Parham.—2nd rev. ed.
            p. cm.
        Contents: v. 1. A guide to mountain biking in western North
Carolina, the Smokies
        ISBN 0-9631861-4-0 (v. 1 : alk paper)
            1. All terrain cycling—United States—Guidebooks. 2. United
States—Guidebooks. I. Title.
        GV1045.P37 1997
        796.6′4′0973—dc21   97-26133
                                                                                CIP
ISBN 1-889596-12-4 (v. 2 3rd rev. ed.: alk paper)

Acknowledgements

As you can see, this book has greatly increased in size (and number of rides) since I wrote the first version back in 1992. One big reason is that there are now more trails available to mountain bikers. Why is this so? It's due largely to the hard work and dedication of certain individuals and advocacy groups in the region.

First and foremost is the Blue Ridge Bicycle Club out of Asheville, N.C. Over the years this club has worked diligently to see that the trails in Pisgah remain open to bikes. From hard physical labor like repairing and building trails to sitting down and talking with forest officials, these folks know how to get a job done. Club members like North Carolina IMBA representative Julie White, trail crew specialist Chuck Ramsey, and many, many others make it all come together.

Another important group is Friends of Dupont State Forest. Ride at Dupont just once and you'll see for yourself what a job these folks have done. The trail system they maintain and were instrumental in creating is one of the best in the Southeast. One individual who stands out in that organization is Woody Keen. Aside from leading monstrous work crews, he's likely to be seen outdoors any day of the week, tidying up a bit of trail, building a bridge, or giving an informal tour of the forest—by bike, of course.

One group of folks commonly left out when it comes to thanks are our national and state forest employees. These dedicated folks love the trails and forest as much as any other user. They listen to us complain and they commonly work side by side with advocacy groups, doing trail maintenance and repair.

For assistance with my work on this new edition, I want to thank Joe Gallwitz from Backcountry Outdoors in Pisgah Forest. Joe, an excellent cyclist who has ridden trails in all 50 states, showed me around Dupont State Forest and made notes to earlier versions of this book based on his contacts with cyclists who used it and frequented his shop.

Special thanks also goes to Blaine Miller, former owner of Carolina Fatz in Asheville. After I potato chipped a front wheel one day in Bent Creek and went to him for help, Blaine did what I think any of the area's great bike shops would have done. He gave me a wheel to use the rest of the day, while he fixed my old one.

Contents

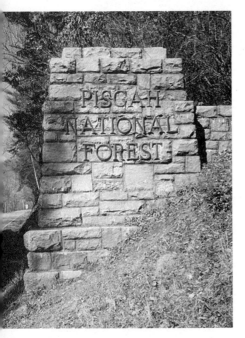

DUPONT STATE FOREST

APPENDIX

WESTSIDE PISGAH AREA

BENT CREEK AREA

Introduction

In 1992 when I wrote the first edition of this book, I felt I had discovered a world-class mountain biking destination. Now, after spending years riding all over the country, I am certain of it.

The Pisgah District of the Pisgah National Forest in western North Carolina is a 157,000-square-mile chunk of land on either side of the Blue Ridge Parkway just west of Asheville, North Carolina. Most folks just call it Pisgah. This is a unique place, with hundreds of miles of designated bike trails that are well marked and well maintained, mountains that rise to over 6,000 ft., waterfalls tumbling from most every stream, enormous rock outcroppings erupting from the dense forest—all this and more in an undeveloped, wild area that is easy to get to. You can find trails that will have you swooshing through dark green tunnels of mountain laurel and rhododendron, and others where you'll splash through streams and wade whitewater rivers. You can ride to the ridge tops and around sheer rock faces and then zoom back down again after seeing stunning views. You'll find backcountry camping, public campgrounds, picnic areas, trailhead parking lots, bike shops and lodging nearby, and good roads to take you from one ride to the next.

It seems that mountain bikers are now discovering what other forest users found out decades ago: Pisgah is a great place to be any time of the year. In summer, the mountains are cool, green and lush. Afternoon thunderstorms are not uncommon. At this time of year you can expect to see fishermen and people floating in inner tubes in the streams. You might see youth groups or families hiking and camping in the backcountry. Some of the trails are designated for horse use as well, and you might encounter equestrians, especially in the South Mills and Avery Creek areas. It is also not uncommon to see climbers on the towering cliffs, meet llama packers, and even encounter the occasional covered wagon.

Fall is leaf season, and it attracts a different crowd. Look for slow driving cars on the forest roads as passengers crane their necks to see splashes of red, yellow and orange on the trees. Fall and early winter are also hunting season. You'll want to wear bright colored clothing, such as blaze orange, at this time of year.

Winter, of course, brings colder temperatures and another well kept secret: Pisgah is a great place to ride in the winter. It doesn't snow too often, especially at the lower elevations. There are no leaves on the trees, so the views are spectacular and unobstructed, and it's not uncommon to have sunny 60-degree days in December, January and February. It might also be cold and rainy, so watch the weather patterns closely before heading into the hills. Fewer people frequent the area at this time so a number of seasonal use trails become available to bikers.

Spring starts sometime in March and goes into May. With it comes new, bright green leaves, thousands of varieties of wildflowers, and people of all types ready to hit the trails. Keeping in mind that Pisgah is a multiuse forest, you can also expect to see timber harvesting, log trucks and maintenance crews any time of the year.

As you ride in Pisgah, you may wonder how the trails stay in such good condition. Credit for this goes to the Asheville area Blue Ridge Bike Club and the Pisgah District's rangers and staff. These folks have done everything right to ensure that trails remain open for mountain bike use. Every month, members of the bike club can be seen out repairing and maintaining sections of trail. District officials monitor the trails and also provide work crews. Pisgah could serve as a model for other trails access groups across the country.

This book lists the best rides in Pisgah. Whether you're a first-time rider or an expert, you'll find rides to suit your tastes and abilities. Study the "How To Use This Book" section on the following pages and choosing the best routes will come easier. Also keep in mind that the Pisgah area is very rugged. Some people find even the easier trails to be difficult.

You'll find a section in the back dedicated to the newly-designated Dupont State Forest. Not quite in Pisgah National Forest, Dupont is so close that those who ride one place will invariably ride at the other. You'll read more about what Dupont has to offer later in this book.

I hope you will have the time, as I have, to give all of these rides a try. You'll be able to see for yourself what a wonderful place Pisgah is to ride a bike.

J.P
March, 2002

Using This Guide

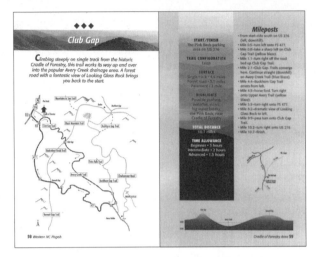

Typical Route Description Pages

- **Route Difficulty** is marked by a series of black diamonds above the route name on the left hand page. One diamond represents the easiest, while five diamonds represents the most difficult of rides. Due to the extreme terrain, you'll find all these routes to be somewhat more difficult than those in other parts of the Southeast.

- Below the **Route Name** is a brief description of the route, followed by a map of the ride.

- **Start/Finish** indicates where the route begins and how to get there.

- **Trail Configuration** describes the type of route.

- There are three **Surface** types: single track (sometimes double track), forest road, and pavement. This will indicate how many miles of each surface to expect.

- In the **Highlights** there will be a one- or two-word description of things you can expect on the trail. For example: Horse use means you may encounter horses, that the trail will have rutted areas with loose rocks, and that any wet places can be very muddy.

- **Total Distance** shows the number of miles you will travel.

- **Time Allowance** is a rough approximation of the time it will take you to ride the trail with minimal stops, according to your ability level.

- **Mileposts** correspond to the adjoining map. The first milepost is at the Start/Finish and is represented by an $\boxed{S}$ on the map. There is a milepost for every turn or any other place of note, and each is represented by a $\boxed{5.3}$ on the map.

- **Maps** are oriented north, with all roads or trails marked by name or number. All roads, trails, buildings, clearings and other features relevant to the route are shown, as well as the best direction of travel. Some of the routes listed in this book can be linked together for shorter or longer rides. When this is the case, those trails or roads are also shown on the map; however, no mileposts or directions are given for these. Maps are not drawn to scale.

- By looking at the **Elevation Profile**, you can get a pretty good idea where the major hills are on the route, how long they will be, and the degree of steepness. It does not show every short rise or dip in the trail.

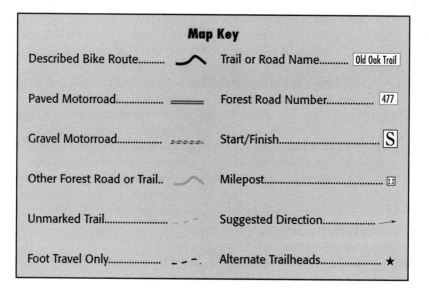

Map Key

Described Bike Route..........	⌒	Trail or Road Name...........	Old Oak Trail
Paved Motorroad.................	══	Forest Road Number.................	477
Gravel Motorroad................	⸱⸱⸱⸱⸱	Start/Finish.......................	$\boxed{S}$
Other Forest Road or Trail..	⌒	Milepost..............................	2.2
Unmarked Trail.....................	‒ ‒	Suggested Direction.................	→
Foot Travel Only..................	⸱ ‒ ⸱	Alternate Trailheads..................	★

Pisgah National Forest

The national forests in North Carolina provide excellent opportunities for mountain bike use. This is especially the case in the Pisgah District of the Pisgah National Forest, where trails are well marked and specifically designated for all uses, including bikes. You'll quickly learn to look for the familiar trail or road markers at all trail heads and trail junctions.

Currently, the trails policy for North Carolina national forests is:

"Driving, riding, possessing, parking or leaving any kind of transportation on a developed trail not designated, and so posted for that specific use" is prohibited. This means that mountain bikes are allowed only on trails posted for their use and any developed trail without such a sign should be considered closed to bikes. Bikes are allowed on gated and closed Forest Service roads, unless posted otherwise.

At the date of this publication, all the trails and roads listed here are open to bikes year-round, with the exception of the seasonal trails. Seasonal trails are open to bikes from October 15 to April 15 only. In the event that excessive resource damage occurs on a specific trail or visitor safety considerations arise, it is possible that some trails will be closed. It is also possible that in the future more trails may be opened or that seasonal trails will be considered for year-round use. Obviously, it is important that all mountain bikers use their best trail etiquette and ride on open trails only. In this way, the good reputation bikers have in Pisgah will be maintained for years to come.

REMEMBER, YOU'RE NOT THE ONLY USER IN THE FOREST

Thousands of people come to Pisgah every year to enjoy the forest. There are bikers, hikers, walkers, horseback riders, hunters, fishermen, sightseers, birders, berry pickers, boys' camps, girls' camps, college groups—the list goes on and on. Each and every user has just as much right to be there as you do. Respect others' rights to the woods and they in turn will respect yours.

HUNTING AND WILDLIFE

Typically, hunting season runs from mid-October through February, with a short turkey season in May. People in these parts enjoy hunting for squirrels, grouse, deer, bear, and turkey, and they have been doing it since before mountain bikes were invented. Likely you'll run into a hunter every now and then, but not too often, as they tend to go where other forest users don't.

The exception to this rule is the last week of November and the first couple of weeks of December, when rifle deer season is open. On nice days at this time of year it can seem as if the woods are teeming with hunters. During these weeks, consider riding in Dupont or at the NC Arboretum, or ride on Sunday

when hunting is not allowed in North Carolina.

If you have any questions concerning the forest, hunting seasons or group camping, contact:

Pisgah District Ranger Office
1001 Pisgah Highway
Pisgah Forest, NC 28768
828-877-3265

Locator Map

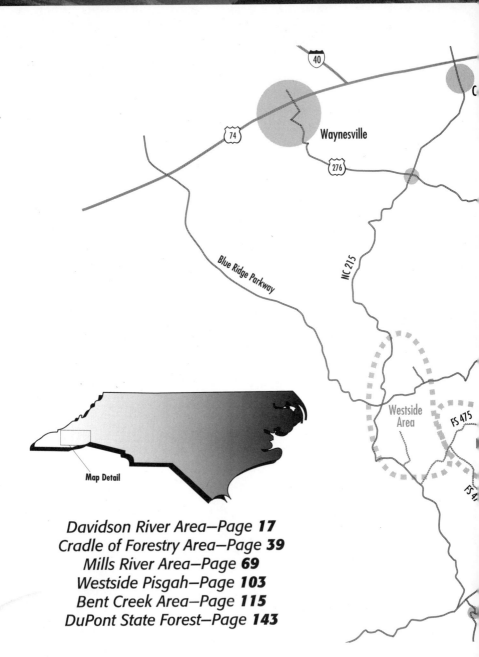

40

74

Waynesville

276

Blue Ridge Parkway

NC 215

FS 475

FS 4

Map Detail

Westside
Area

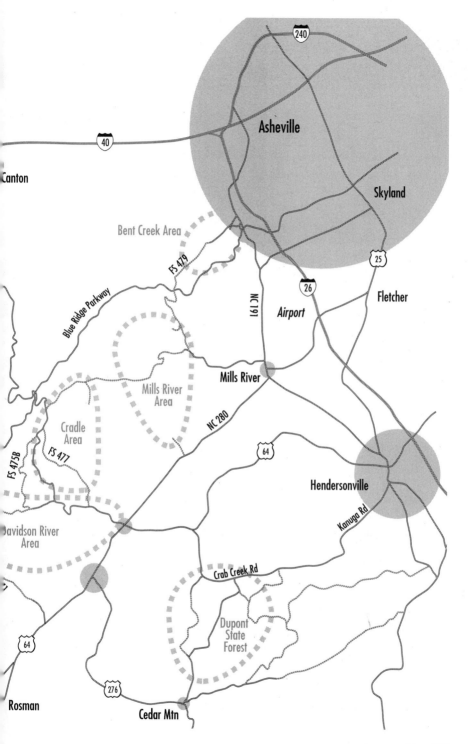

Trail Advocacy

When mountain biking first came on the scene in the southeastern United States back in the late 1980s, people could ride their bikes on almost any trail. To see a cyclists on a "foot" trail was a novelty for most people. As the sport took off in the early 1990s, the novelty quickly wore off and the more traditional user groups began claiming turf. Near metropolitan areas where the number of trail users was high, conflicts were inevitable. Threats of those conflicts eventually spread to the remotest portions of the forest as land managers began taking hard looks at what trails were suitable for which user groups.

Now, more than a decade later mountain bikers have learned a lot of valuable lessons. Bicycle clubs have evolved to include trail advocacy directors and work crews. Some even have thousands of dollars worth of trail building tools. Most every weekend, somewhere in the Southeast there's a group of cyclists out repairing or building a trail. The organization all these folks look to (and most are members of) is the International Mountain Biking Association (IMBA). IMBA's mission is to promote environmentally sound and socially responsible biking. IMBA does everything from sending paid trail crew specialists across the country, to sponsoring trail work camps, to lobbying land managers on the national and international level.

RULES OF THE TRAIL

- **Ride on open trails only.**
  Respect trail and road closures, and avoid possible trespass on private land. Federal and state wilderness areas are closed to cycling. The way you ride will influence trail management decisions and policies.

- **Leave no trace.** Be sensitive to the dirt beneath you. Many trails in this part of North Carolina can become quite muddy after periods of prolonged rain or freeze-thaw conditions. Consider riding on the hard packed forest roads at these times.

- **Control your bicycle.** Inattention for even a second can cause problems. Don't create danger for yourself and other trail users.

- **Always yield trail.** Make known your approach well in advance. A friendly greeting is considerate and works well; don't startle others. Show your respect when passing by slowing to a walking pace or even stopping. Anticipate meeting other trail users around corners and in blind spots.

- **Never spook animals.** When passing horses, use special care and follow directions from the horseback riders (ask if uncertain). Always ride slowly and quietly through areas where wildlife may be feeding or nesting.

- **Plan ahead.** Know your equipment, your ability and the area in which you are riding—and prepare accordingly. Always wear a helmet.

MORE INFORMATION

For more information or to join any of these trail advocacy groups, contact below:

- **IMBA**
  P.O. Box 7578
  Boulder, CO 80306
  303-545-9011
  www.imba.org

- **Blue Ridge Bicycle Club**
  PO Box 309
  Asheville, NC 28802
  www.blueridgebicycleclub.org

- **Friends of Dupont State Forest**
  PO Box 42
  Hendersonville, NC 28793
  trailboss@dupontforest.com
  www.dupontforest.com

Davidson River Area

Driving out of the towns of Brevard and Pisgah Forest on US 276 into the Pisgah National Forest can be shocking. Immediately you trade traffic lights and store fronts for the calm, cool, quiet of the forest. This is the Davidson River area, home to some of Pisgah's more notable features and landmarks. Just up the road is the District Ranger Office and also Davidson River Campground. The Davidson River itself parallels the highway, and depending on the season you're sure to spot fly-fishermen, tubers, or picnickers enjoying its sparkling waters.

Farther on is Looking Glass Falls, a favorite tourist stop, right by the road. You owe it to yourself to stop here too; it's quite a sight.

Along the upper reaches of the Davidson is the Pisgah Forest State Fish Hatchery. Here several varieties of mountain trout are reared, and eventually they stock mountain streams throughout western North Carolina. Right next door is the Pisgah Center for Wildlife Education. If you have the time, make sure to pay a visit here as well. It's a great place to learn about the wildlife you may encounter while out on the trail. You can also learn more about some of the more traditional recreational uses of the forest, such as hunting and fishing.

Towering above the area is Looking Glass Rock, a domed mountain top famous for its sheer
(continues)

Davidson River Area

granite walls. It's a rock climber's paradise and for the rest of us, something wonderful to see. Looking Glass, John Rock and Cedar Rock Mountain loom over the area as well. You can hike to the top of them, but you'll have to leave your bike at the bottom.

As for mountain biking, this area is tops. Trails range from fairly easy (as Pisgah standards go) to very difficult. Since this area is so close to the Forest entrance, it understandably sees a lot of use. Expect to see hikers and other bikers on the trails. In summer, you're likely to run into a camp group or two. Note that a few of these trails are only open to bikes during the cooler months. You should find all of the trailheads easily accessible. In fact, except for one, they are all just off a paved road.

I've given you nine routes to choose from in this area. A number of them start and end in the same place, so you can do them as is or make up your own combinations of varying degrees of difficulty. Whichever you choose, you're sure to enjoy them.

Thrift Cove
Sycamore Cove
North Slope
Pressley Gap
Gumstand Gap
Butter Gap
Picklesimer Fields
Daniel Ridge
Farlow Gap

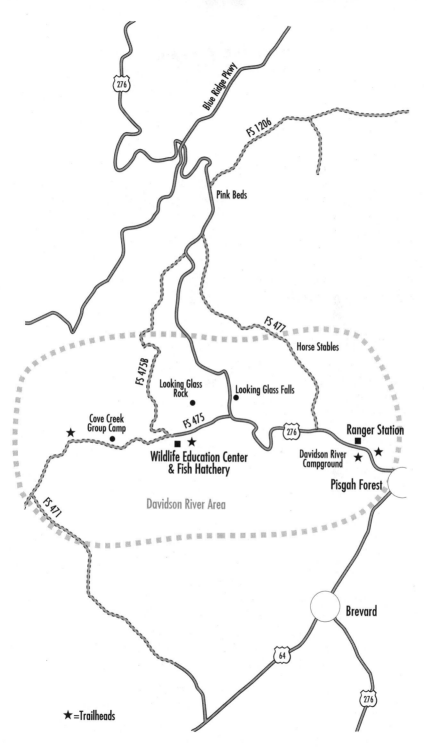

★ =Trailheads

Thrift Cove

Only minutes from the ranger station, this trail works its way slowly up the Black Mountain Trail before making a long descent down a grassy logging road and back to the trailhead. You can double your distance by combining this ride with the Sycamore Cove Trail via Grass Road.

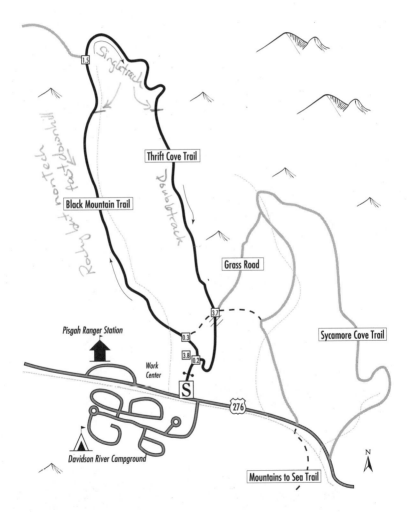

START/FINISH
Black Mountain
trailhead parking, just
south of Pisgah District
Ranger Station on
U.S. 276

TRAIL CONFIGURATION
Loop

SURFACE
Single track • 4 miles

HIGHLIGHTS
Grassy surface, fern
glades, meadows, mud
bogs, rhododendron
tunnels, open woods

TOTAL DISTANCE
4 miles

TIME ALLOWANCE
Beginner • 1.5 hours
Intermediate • 1 hour
Advanced • 30 minutes

Mileposts

- From start–ride out the back side
  of the parking area and around
  the gate.
- Mile 0.2–turn left onto Black
  Mountain Trail (white blaze).
- Mile 0.3–Mountains to Sea Trail
  exits right. Continue up Black
  Mountain Trail.
- Mile 1.5–bear right onto Thrift
  Cove Trail (red blaze).
- Mile 3.7–Grass Road exits left and
  100 yds. farther down, the
  Mountains to Sea Trail crosses.
  Continue straight down through
  meadow to remain on Thrift Cove
  Trail.
- Mile 3.8–bear left at jct. of Black
  Mountain Trail.
- Mile 4–finish.

★=Start

US 276
FS 477
Ranger Station
Davidson R.
Campground
Sycamore Flats
NC 280
Pisgah Forest
Brevard
US 64

Black Mtn/Thrift Jct

2000'
1000'

Sycamore Cove

his is the first trail you come to as you enter the national forest from Brevard on US 276. It climbs quickly up through a fern glade to the ridgeline and then rolls slowly downward along the ridge on an old road bed before dropping suddenly back to the highway.

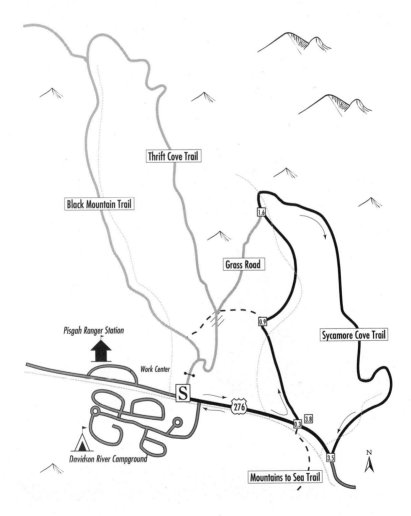

Thrift Cove Trail

Black Mountain Trail

1.6

Grass Road

Pisgah Ranger Station

0.9

Sycamore Cove Trail

Work Center

S

276

3.8

0.3

Davidson River Campground

3.5

N

Mountains to Sea Trail

START/FINISH
Black Mountain trailhead parking, just south of Pisgah District Ranger Station on US 276

TRAIL CONFIGURATION
Loop

SURFACE
Single track • 3.2 miles
Pavement • 0.9

HIGHLIGHTS
Log bridges, ridge riding, rhododendron tunnels, log steps, steep downhill

TOTAL DISTANCE
4.1 miles

TIME ALLOWANCE
Beginner • 1.5 hours
Intermediate • 1.25 hrs
Advanced • 45 minutes

Mileposts

- From start–ride south (left) on US 276.
- Mile 0.3–turn left onto Sycamore Cove Trail (blue blaze). The Mountains to Sea Trail shares this trail for a ways, so you will also see a round white blaze.
- Mile 0.9–Mountains to Sea Trail exits to left. Stay on Sycamore Cove Trail.
- Mile 1.6–Grass Road enters from left. Stay on Sycamore Cove Trail.
- Mile 3.5–turn right on US 276.
- Mile 4.1–finish.

★ =Start

US 276
FS 477
Ranger Station
Davidson R. Campground
Sycamore Flats
NC 280
Pisgah Forest
Brevard
US 64

Jct Grass Road

2000'
1000'

North Slope

*W*ith its short but steep hills, this trail is great by itself, or it can be a nice addition to any of the rides leaving from the district ranger station.

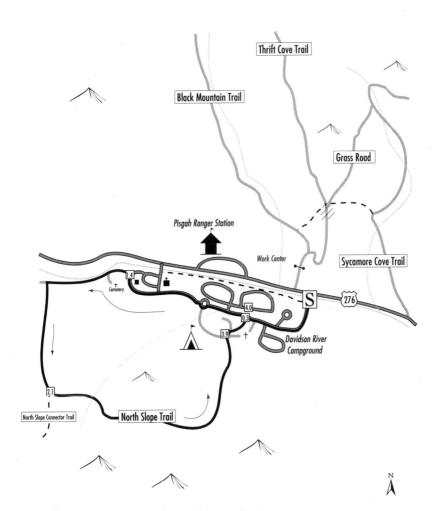

START/FINISH
Art Loeb Trailhead parking lot just off U.S. 276 at entrance to Davidson River Campground.

TRAIL CONFIGURATION
Loop w/ extension

SURFACE
Single track • 4 miles
Pavement • 0.3 miles

HIGHLIGHTS
Spotty views, Davidson River, short steep uphill, ridge ride, rhododendron tunnels, mud bog

TOTAL DISTANCE
4.3 miles

TIME ALLOWANCE
Beginner • 1.5 hours
Intermediate • 1 hour
Advanced • 40 minutes

SEASONAL TRAIL
OPEN OCT 15 – APR 15

Mileposts
- From start–ride across Davidson River, past the Exercise Trail and into Davidson River Campground.
- Mile 0.3–Pass the amphitheater parking area and start the loop. Continue through the campground to the last bath house.
- Mile 1.4–turn left onto the North Slope Trail. Follow the orange blazes along the river past the cemetery and then take a sharp left up the hill.
- Mile 2.1–North Slope Connector Trail enters from right. Stay to left on North Slope Trail.
- Mile 3.9–almost back to campground. Several trails go in all directions. Watch for orange blazes.
- Mile 4.0–Amphitheater parking area. Turn right and head out of campground.
- Mile 4.3–finish.

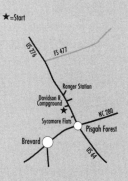

★ =Start

US 276 FS 477

Ranger Station

Davidson R.
Campground

Sycamore Flats

NC 280

Pisgah Forest

Brevard

US 64

Jct North Slope Tr

North Slope

2000'

1000'

Pressley Gap

Starting and finishing at the ranger station, this ride combines easy streamside riding with a four-mile climb and good technical downhill single track.

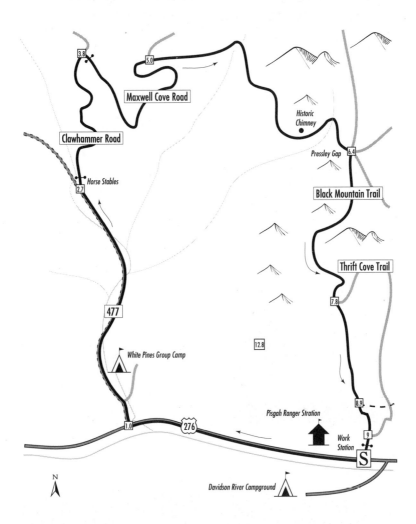

Maxwell Cove Road

Clawhammer Road

Historic Chimney

Pressley Gap | 6.4

3.8

5.0

Horse Stables | 2.7

Black Mountain Trail

Thrift Cove Trail

7.8

477

White Pines Group Camp

12.8

8.9

Pisgah Ranger Station

Work Station | 9

S

1.0

276

N

Davidson River Campground

START/FINISH
Black Mountain trailhead parking, just south of Pisgah District Ranger Station on US 276

TRAIL CONFIGURATION
Loop

SURFACE
Single track • 2.9 miles
Double track • 1.4 miles
Forest road • 4 miles
Pavement • 1 mile

HIGHLIGHTS
Views, timber cuts, some horse use, grassy road, diagonal log water breaks, short pushes

TOTAL DISTANCE
9.3 miles

TIME ALLOWANCE
Beginner • 5 hours
Intermediate • 3.5 hours
Advanced • 2.5 hours

Mileposts

- From start–ride west on FS 276.
- Mile 1.0–turn right onto FS 477. You should see a sign pointing to the horseback riding area.
- Mile 2.7–horse stables. Turn right on gated Clawhammer Road.
- Mile 3.8–turn right onto gated Maxwell Cove Road.
- Mile 5.0–unmarked road to left. Continue right up Maxwell Cove Road (it becomes grassy).
- Mile 6.4–Pressley Gap. 5-way junction. Take a sharp right onto Black Mountain/Mountains to Sea Trail (white blaze w/ white dot).
- Mile 7.8–Thrift Cove Trail enters from left.
- Mile 8.9–Mountains to Sea Trail exits to left.
- Mile 9.0–Thrift Cove Trail enters from left.
- Mile 9.3–finish.

★ =Start

US 276 · FS 477

Ranger Station

Davidson R. Campground

Sycamore Flats

NC 280

Pisgah Forest

Brevard

US 64

Pressley Gap

Horse Stables

3000'

2000'

1000'

Gumstand Gap

With views of Looking Glass Rock, John Rock and several high waterfalls, this is an appealing scenic ride. Throw in four miles of great single track and you've got something special.

Rode as a Out-N-Back. Mostly Wide Track with Several Small Stream Crossings on Logs.

3.7

4.6   225

Caney Bottom Extension Trail

5.1

Caney Bottom Loop Trail

Looking Glass Rock

Cove Creek Falls

Caney Bottom Loop Trail

Slick Rock Falls

475B

7.3

Cove Creek Group Camp

475

9.3   0.2

7.8   7.9

Davidson River Trail

Fish Hatchery

Wildlife Education Center

S

John Rock

N

START/FINISH
State Fish Hatchery and Wildlife Center on FS 475

TRAIL CONFIGURATION
Loop

SURFACE
Single track • 4 miles
Forest road • 5.8 miles

HIGHLIGHTS
Rhododendron tunnels, waterfalls, cliff views, creek crossings, heavy use causes mud in the rainy season

TOTAL DISTANCE
9.8 miles

TIME ALLOWANCE
Beginner • 2.5 hours
Intermediate • 1.75 hrs
Advanced • 1.25 hours

Mileposts

- From start–cross bridge and turn left out of fish hatchery parking lot onto FS 475.
- Mile 0.2–turn right onto FS 475B.
- Mile 3.7–Gumstand Gap. Turn left onto FS 225. In the next mile, numerous unmarked roads and trails will enter on either side. Stay on FS 225.
- Mile 4.6–turn left onto gated road. This is the Caney Bottom Extension Trail (marked by a sign). Go 50 yards and the trail forks off to the right (yellow blazes). Turn right onto the trail.
- Mile 5.1–Caney Bottom Trail. Turn right (blue blazes).
- Mile 7.3–bypass Cove Cr Group Camp. Turn right onto road.
- Mile 7.8–turn left onto FS 475, then right on Davidson River Trail (blue blazes).
- Mile 7.9–turn right on Davidson River Trail.
- Mile 9.3–bear right on FS 475.
- Mile 9.8–finish.

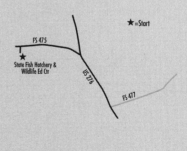

Gumstand Gap   Caney Bottom Ext Tr

Butter Gap

*A*fter a long climb on forest roads you'll find a wide trail up to Butter Gap and the foot of Cedar Rock's cliffs. Check your brake cables, because the last 3.5 miles are all downhill!

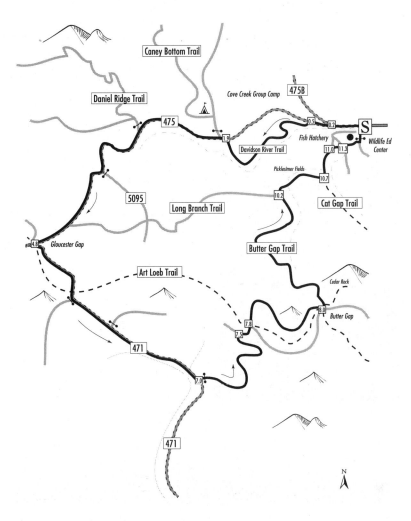

START/FINISH
State Fish Hatchery and Wildlife Center on FS 475

TRAIL CONFIGURATION
Loop

SURFACE
Single track • 5.5 miles
Forest road • 6.3 miles

HIGHLIGHTS
Spotty views, Cedar Rock, waterfall, technical sections

TOTAL DISTANCE
11.8 miles

TIME ALLOWANCE
Beginner • 4 hours
Intermediate • 2.5 hours
Advanced • 1.75 hours

SEASONAL TRAIL
OPEN OCT 15 – APR 15

Mileposts

- From start–cross bridge and turn left onto FS 475.
- Mile 0.2–bear left; stay on FS 475.
- Mile 0.5–turn left onto Davidson River Trail (blue blaze).
- Mile 1.9–turn left on FS 475.
- Mile 4.8–Gloucester Gap. Turn left onto FS 471.
- Mile 7.0–Turn left onto unmarked gated road. This is the second gated road on the left after crossing the Art Loeb Trail. It quickly becomes a trail.
- Mile 7.5–bear right at trail fork past old gate.
- Mile 7.8–5-way jct. of trails. Cross Art Loeb and head around north side of ridge.
- Mile 8.0–Butter Gap. 7-way jct. of trails. Turn sharply to left downhill on Butter Gap Trail (blue blaze).
- Mile 10.2–Long Branch Trail enters left. Bear right.
- Mile 10.7–pass through Picklesimer Fields and turn left onto Cat Gap Trail (orange blaze).
- Mile 11.0–bear right at trail fork.
- Mile 11.3– cross gravel road and then a footbridge.
- Mile 11.8–turn left to finish.

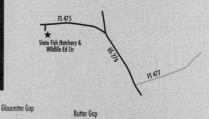

Gloucester Gap   Butter Gap

3000'
2000'
1000'

Picklesimer Fields

*W*ith equal amounts of single track and gravel roads, this is quite the ride. You'll enjoy testing your skills on the log bridges and rutted hills while taking in views of John Rock, several waterfalls and, of course, Picklesimer Fields.

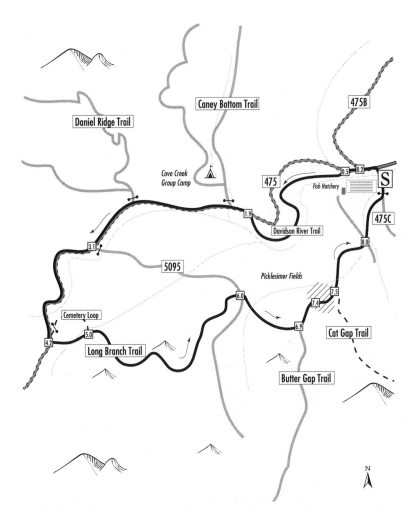

START/FINISH
State Fish Hatchery and Wildlife Center on FS 475

TRAIL CONFIGURATION
Loop

SURFACE
Single track • 4.2 miles
Forest road • 4.2 miles

HIGHLIGHTS
Long uphill on gravel road, rhododendron tunnels, rutted trail, log bridges, rock slabs, waterfalls and cascades, views

TOTAL DISTANCE
8.4 miles

TIME ALLOWANCE
Beginner • 2.5 hours
Intermediate • 2 hours
Advanced • 1.25 hours

SEASONAL TRAIL
OPEN OCT 15 – APR 15

Mileposts

- From start–cross bridge and turn left onto FS 475.
- Mile 0.2–stay on FS 475.
- Mile 0.5–turn left on Davidson River Trail (blue blaze).
- Mile 1.9–turn left on FS 475.
- Mile 3.1–gated FS 5095 on left.. Continue on FS 475.
- Mile 4.2–Cemetery Loop Trail. enters on left. Continue 100 yds.. farther and turn left onto Long Branch Trail (orange blaze).
- Mile 5.0–jct. Cemetery Loop Trail. Stay right on Long Branch Trail.
- Mile 6.0–cross logging road.
- Mile 6.9–turn left on Butter Gap Trail (blue blaze).
- Mile 7.4–Picklesimer Fields.
- Mile 7.5–turn left on Cat Gap Trail (orange blaze).
- Mile 8.0–cross gravel road and then a footbridge.
- Mile 8.4–turn left to finish.

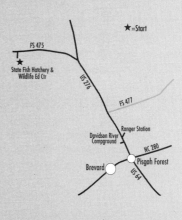

★=Start

FS 475
State Fish Hatchery & Wildlife Ed Ctr
US 276
FS 477
Ranger Station
Davidson River Campground
NC 280
Brevard
Pisgah Forest
US 64

Long Branch Tr   Picklesimer Fields

3000'
2000'
1000'

2000

Daniel Ridge

It's a bit of a push to the ridge, but once you're there the extra effort is long forgotten. The grassy woods, open meadows and cliff-top views heighten your senses, while some technical riding sharpens your skills.

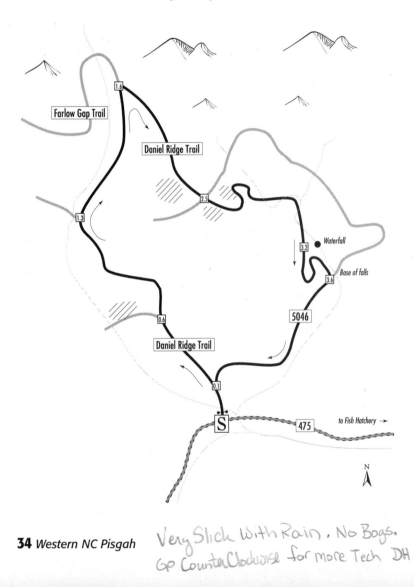

Very Slick With Rain, No Bogs.
Go CounterClockwise for more Tech DH

START/FINISH
Parking area 0.8 miles west of entrance to Cove Creek Group Camp on FS 475

TRAIL CONFIGURATION
Loop

SURFACE
Single track • 3.5 miles
Forest road • 0.6 miles

HIGHLIGHTS
Roots, log bridges, waterfall, steep hills, mud bogs, short push, grassy woods, meadows

TOTAL DISTANCE
4.1 miles

TIME ALLOWANCE
Beginner • 2 hours
Intermediate • 1.25 hrs
Advanced • 45 minutes

Mileposts

- From start–ride through gate on unmarked FS 137.
- Mile 0.1–cross bridge, go 25 yds. and turn left onto Daniel Ridge Trail (red blazes).
- Mile 0.6–trail forks. Take the right fork.
- Mile 1.3–trail forks just before old log bridge. Take right fork up hill (red blazes). The next 0.3 miles is pretty steep.
- Mile 1.6–turn right at jct. of Farlow Gap Trail. You are still on the Daniel Ridge Trail (red blazes).
- Mile 2.5–cross logging road.
- Mile 3.2–look and listen for waterfall to left of trail.
- Mile 3.6–turn right onto FS 5046.
- Mile 4.1–finish.

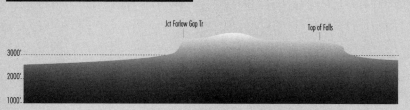

Farlow Gap

*This is not a ride for someone with bad knees. A long climb is followed by a great ride along the ridge and then a **very** steep downhill that for most folks requires a fair amount of carrying.*

Farlow Gap Trail

Daniel Ridge Trail

Farlow Gap

Art Loeb Trail

Long Branch Trail

to Fish Hatchery

Gloucester Gap

START/FINISH
Parking area 0.8 miles west of entrance to Cove Creek Group Camp on FS 475

TRAIL CONFIGURATION
Loop

SURFACE
Single track • 5.6 miles
Forest road • 4.8 miles

HIGHLIGHTS
Great views, 5-mile uphill, very steep and rocky downhill, lots of waterfalls

TOTAL DISTANCE
10.4 miles

TIME ALLOWANCE
Beginner • not advised
Intermediate • 4.5 hours
Advanced • 3 hours

Mileposts

- From start–ride southwest on FS 475.
- Mile 2.2–Gloucester Gap. Turn right onto FS 229.
- Mile 4.8–road forks, with dirt barricades on each fork. Take the left (upper) fork up rocky old road bed.
- Mile 5.0–Art Loeb/Mountains to Sea Trail enters left.
- Mile 5.1–Art Loeb/Mountains to Sea Trail exits left.
- Mile 6.1–Farlow Gap. Trails jct. here. Turn right onto Farlow Gap Trail (blue blaze).
- Mile 6.8–very steep downhill to waterfall.
- Mile 8.6–turn right on Daniel Ridge Trail (red blaze).
- Mile 9.0–old wide log bridge on right. Bear left on Daniel Ridge Trail (red blaze).
- Mile 9.6–trail to field bears off to right. Stay left
- Mile 10.3–turn right onto forest road.
- Mile 10.4–finish.

Cradle of Forestry Area

Pisgah is the birthplace of modern forestry in America. It was in the region just south of the Blue Ridge Parkway and off US 276 that the first school of forestry was created over 100 years ago. This is why it is known today as The Cradle of Forestry. For nearly as far as the eye can see, this land was once owned by George W. Vanderbilt— the Vanderbilt who was the original owner of the Biltmore House in Asheville. Vanderbilt also owned a considerable amount of land. In his day, it was a devastated tract of logged-out forest. Vanderbilt believed that the land could be restored, and he hired for that job a man named Gifford Pinchot.

It was Pinchot, and later Dr. Carl Schenck, who put into practice the idea of forest conservation and multiple use in the Pisgah area. Schenck is credited with starting the forestry school, and Pinchot would go on to be the first chief of the US Forest Service. When riding in this area, make time to visit Pisgah's Forest Discovery Center located on the original site of the former school. Here you can learn much more about forestry practices new and old, as well as the forest itself.

That's how the area got its name, but it's famous for other things as well, and you'll find a *(continues)*

Cradle of Forestry Area

number of forest "attractions" that can add to any mountain biking adventure. Just south of the Forest Discovery Center is Sliding Rock. Children of all ages have been enjoying this natural water slide for generations. Even Dr. Schenck's forestry students stole away on a hot afternoon to recreate here. Be sure to give it a try yourself—it's a real hoot!

Just north of the Discovery Center is an area called The Pink Beds. Visit here anytime from late May to early July and you'll learn how it got its name. Mountain Laurel and Rhododendron bloom in such quantities, the woods become pink.

As for riding, this area is excellent. Except for the rather flat shelf of the Pink Beds, the terrain is quite rugged. Trails climb to knife-like ridges where you'll have panoramic views of the surrounding mountains. Looking Glass Rock almost always comes into view, and using it as a landmark, you can begin to pick out other peaks. Other trails take you over the mountains to the upper reaches of the South Mills River. Odds are you'll enjoy any one you choose.

Twin Falls
Buckhorn Gap
Clawhammer
Bennett Gap
Perry Cove
Buckwheat Knob
Coontree Gap
The Pink Beds
Club Gap
Cradle Loop
Mountains to Mills River
Squirrel Gap
Horse Cove Gap

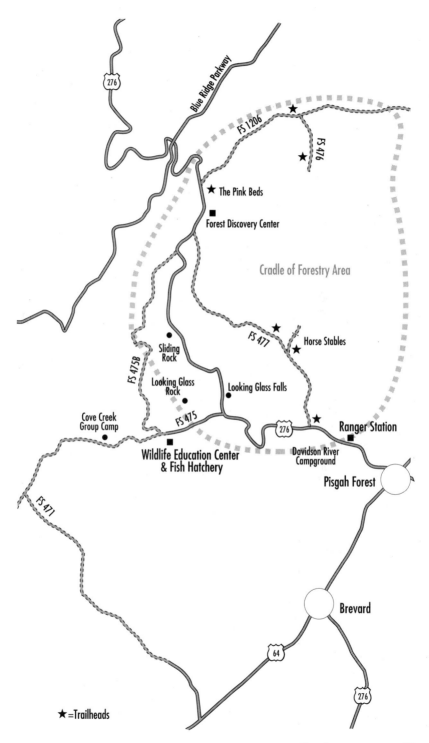

276

Blue Ridge Parkway

FS 1206

FS 476

★ The Pink Beds

■ Forest Discovery Center

Cradle of Forestry Area

FS 477

★ Horse Stables
★

★
Sliding
Rock

● Looking Glass
Rock

FS 475B

FS 475

● Looking Glass Falls

Cove Creek
Group Camp
●

■
Wildlife Education Center
& Fish Hatchery

276

★ Ranger Station
■

Davidson River
Campground

Pisgah Forest

FS 471

Brevard

64

276

★ =Trailheads

Twin Falls

A gem in the Avery Creek system. You'll double your visual pleasure as this ride takes you within a short hike of a double waterfall. Two creeks tumble over a cliff side by side.

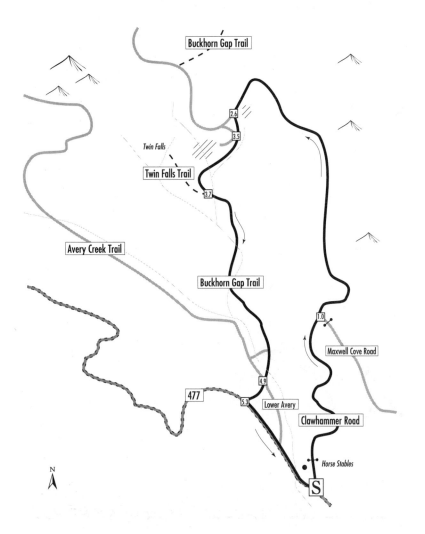

Buckhorn Gap Trail

2.6

3.5

Twin Falls

Twin Falls Trail

3.7

Avery Creek Trail

Buckhorn Gap Trail

1.0

Maxwell Cove Road

4.9

477

5.3

Lower Avery

Clawhammer Road

Horse Stables

N

S

START/FINISH
Horseback riding area
on FS 477
1.5 miles north of White
Pines Group Camp

TRAIL CONFIGURATION
Loop

SURFACE
Single track • 2.7 miles
Forest road • 3.4 miles

HIGHLIGHTS
Views, twin waterfalls,
log bridges, few short
carries, horse fords, long
uphill on gravel road,
horse use

TOTAL DISTANCE
6.1 miles

TIME ALLOWANCE
Beginner • 3 hours
Intermediate • 2 hours
Advanced • 1.5 hours

Mileposts

- From start–ride through gate up Clawhammer Road.
- Mile 1.0–Maxwell Cove Road enters from right. Stay left on Clawhammer Road.
- Mile 2.6–a grassy meadow (old cemetery) on the left marks the entrance onto Buckhorn Gap Trail. Turn left down grassy road bed (orange blazes).
- Mile 3.5–Buckhorn Gap Trail goes in two directions off road bed. Turn left down the creek following orange blazes.
- Mile 3.7–hiker-only trail to Twin Falls turns off to right. Leave your bike here to make the short hike to the falls.
- Mile 4.9–ford creek and jct. Avery Creek Trail. Take Upper Avery Creek Trail to the right (yellow blaze).
- Mile 5.3–turn left onto FS 477 (downhill).
- Mile 6.1–finish.

★ =Start

Horse Stables

FS 477

US 276

Ranger Station

Davidson R.
Campground

NC 280

Pisgah Forest

Brevard

US 64

Jct Buckhorn Gap Tr   Twin Falls   Cross Avery Cr

3000'

2000'

1000'

Buckhorn Gap

If you can take the four-mile climb at the beginning in stride, you'll love the ridge ride that follows. In places the mountain falls off on both sides only a few feet from the trail.

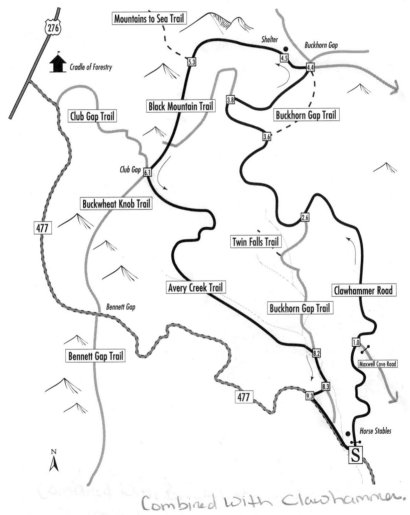

Mountains to Sea Trail

Shelter

Buckhorn Gap

276

Cradle of Forestry

5.3

4.5

4.4

Black Mountain Trail

3.8

Buckhorn Gap Trail

Club Gap Trail

3.6

Club Gap   6.1

Buckwheat Knob Trail

477

2.6

Twin Falls Trail

Avery Creek Trail

Clawhammer Road

Bennett Gap

Buckhorn Gap Trail

Bennett Gap Trail

1.0

8.2

Maxwell Cove Road

8.3

477   9.3

Horse Stables

S

N

Combined With Clawhammer.

START/FINISH
Horseback riding area
on FS 477
1.5 miles north of White
Pines Group Camp

TRAIL CONFIGURATION
Loop

SURFACE
Single track • 4.9 miles
Forest road • 5.2 miles

HIGHLIGHTS
Great views, horse use,
log bridges, ridge riding,
Buckhorn Gap Shelter,
waterfalls, mud bogs

TOTAL DISTANCE
10.1 miles

TIME ALLOWANCE
Beginner • 4 hours
Intermediate • 3 hours
Advanced • 2 hours

Mileposts

- From start–ride through gate up Clawhammer Road.
- Mile 1.0–Maxwell Cove Road enters from right.
- Mile 2.6–Buckhorn Gap Trail enters from left.
- Mile 3.6–Buckhorn Gap Trail exits to right.
- Mile 3.8–unmarked road enters left. Bear right.
- Mile 4.4–Buckhorn Gap. Jct. Black Mountain/Mountains to Sea Trail and Buckhorn Gap Trail. Turn left up steps onto Black Mountain/Mountains to Sea Trail (white blazes).
- Mile 4.5–Buckhorn Gap Shelter.
- Mile 5.3–Mountains to Sea Trail exits to right.
- Mile 6.1–Club Gap. Turn left onto Avery Creek Trail (blue blazes).
- Mile 8.2–Buckhorn Gap Trail enters from left.
- Mile 8.3–horse ford. Turn right onto Upper Avery Creek Trail (yellow blazes).
- Mile 9.3–turn left onto FS 477.
- Mile 10.1– finish.

★=Start   Horse Stables

US 276   FS 477

Ranger Station

Davidson R.
Campground   NC 280

Pisgah Forest

Buckhorn Gap   Club Gap

4000'

3000'

2000'

Clawhammer

*T*his ride will hammer you. You'll start with a six-mile climb, the last 1.5 miles of which is a push up steep rock steps. The cliff-top view at the highest point is pretty spectacular—the perfect reward for going the distance.

Shelter   Buckhorn Gap

4.4

3.8

Buckhorn Gap Trail

5.6

Black Mountain Trail

Twin Falls Trail

Turkey Pen Gap Trail

6.2

Buckhorn Gap Trail

Clawhammer Road

Avery Creek Trail

9.6 1.0

Maxwell Cove Road

Historic Chimney

477

Pressley Gap

7.2

Horse Stables

S

N

Combined with Buckhorn gap. Went CounterClockwise. Lots of Pushing. Go Clockwise

Mileposts

- From start–ride through gate up Clawhammer Road.
- Mile 1.0–Maxwell Cove Road exits to right.
- Mile 3.8–unmarked road enters left. Bear right.
- Mile 4.4–Buckhorn Gap. 5-way trail junction. Turn right onto Black Mountain/Mountains to Sea Trail (white blaze w/ white dot).
- Mile 5.6–spectacular cliff-top view.
- Mile 6.2–Turkey Pen Gap Trail. (blue blaze) enters from left. Stay on Black Mountain Trail (white blaze).
- Mile 7.2–Pressley Gap and another 5-way interchange of trails. Take a sharp right down grassy Maxwell Cove Road. Check your speed; there may be horses on their way up.
- Mile 9.6–turn left onto Clawhammer Road.
- Mile 10.7–finish.

START/FINISH
Horseback riding area on FS 477
1.5 miles north of White Pines Group Camp

TRAIL CONFIGURATION
Loop w/ extension

SURFACE
Single track • 2.8 miles
Double track • 1.4 miles
Forest road • 6.5 miles

HIGHLIGHTS
Long climb, technical uphill, great views, rock cave, rhododendron tunnel, horse use

TOTAL DISTANCE
10.7 miles

TIME ALLOWANCE
Beginner • 4+ hours
Intermediate • 3 hours
Advanced • 2 hours

★ =Start   Horse Stables
US 276   FS 477
Ranger Station
Davidson R.
Campground   NC 280
Pisgah Forest
Brevard   US 64

Cliff View   Jct Turkey Pen Gap Tr
Buckhorn Gp
4000'
3000'
2000'

Bennett Gap

After a grunt of a climb you'll find a trail that snakes along the top of a knife-like ridge with cliff-top views of Looking Glass Rock and Clawhammer Mountain. Short sections are so technical it seems as if your wheels will barely hang on. The ride to the bottom is a hoot.

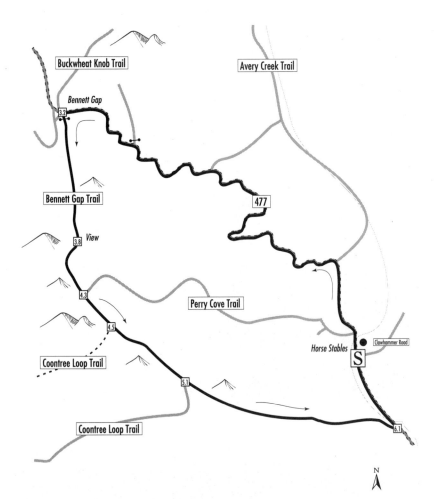

Buckwheat Knob Trail

Avery Creek Trail

Bennett Gap

3.2

Bennett Gap Trail

477

3.8 View

4.3

Perry Cove Trail

4.5

Horse Stables Clawhammer Road

S

Coontree Loop Trail

5.1

Coontree Loop Trail

6.1

N

Mileposts

- From start–ride uphill on FS 477.
- Mile 3.2–Bennett Gap. Turn left onto Bennett Gap Trail (red blaze).
- Mile 3.8–cliff-top view of Looking Glass Rock.
- Mile 4.3–Perry Cove Trail exits downhill on the left..
- Mile 4.5–Coontree Loop Trail enters from right and shares this trail.
- Mile 5.1–Coontree Loop Trail exits to right. Stay left.
- Mile 6.1–turn left onto FS 477.
- Mile 6.5–finish.

START/FINISH
Horseback riding area on FS 477
1.5 miles north of White Pines Group Camp

TRAIL CONFIGURATION
Loop

SURFACE
Single track • 2.9 miles
Forest road • 3.6 miles

HIGHLIGHTS
Long climb, technical rocky sections, views

TOTAL DISTANCE
6.5 miles

TIME ALLOWANCE
Beginner • 3 hours
Intermediate • 1.75 hrs
Advanced • 1 hour

SEASONAL TRAIL
OPEN OCT 15 – APR 15

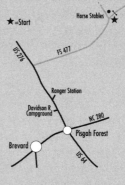

★ =Start

Horse Stables

US 276

FS 477

Ranger Station

Davidson R.
Campground

NC 280

Pisgah Forest

Brevard

US 64

Cliff-top View

Jct Coontree Tr

3000'
2000'
1000'

Perry Cove

*T*his ride starts out exactly the same as the Bennett Gap ride by climbing steadily up to a clifftop view. From there the downhill adventure begins. Experts will love trying to clean the first rocky pitch, and the descent into Perry Cove is tight, smooth and steep. Going down is so much faster than going up.

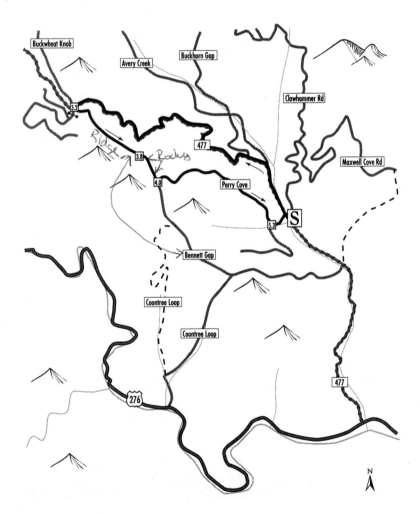

START/FINISH
Horseback riding area
on FS 477
1.5 miles north of White
Pines Group Camp

TRAIL CONFIGURATION
Loop

SURFACE
Single track • 2.3 miles
Forest road • 3.2 miles

HIGHLIGHTS
Forest road climb,
spectacular cliff-top
view, technical rocky
descent, steep narrow
trail, wildlife fields

TOTAL DISTANCE
5.5 miles

TIME ALLOWANCE
Beginner • 3 hours
Intermediate • 2 hours
Advanced • 1 hour

SEASONAL TRAIL
OPEN OCT 15 – APR 15

Mileposts

- From start–ride north on FS 477.
- Mile 3.2–turn left on Bennett Gap Trail.
- Mile 3.8–cliff-top view of Looking Glass Rock and other prominent Pisgah landmarks.
- Mile 4–there's a steep, rocky, technical descent to here. Turn left on Perry Cove Trail (orange blaze).
- Mile 5.3–bottom out at jct. of old logging road. Bear left and then a ways farther, bear right on FS 477.
- Mile 5.5–finish.

Buckwheat Knob

he first three miles is mostly uphill and it takes some pushing to get over Buckwheat Knob, but the descent to the creek is a real treat. You'll enjoy the views from the gravel road.

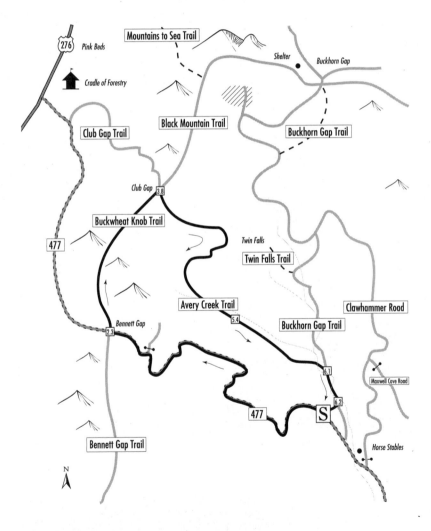

276 Pink Beds

Mountains to Sea Trail

Shelter

Buckhorn Gap

Cradle of Forestry

Club Gap Trail

Black Mountain Trail

Buckhorn Gap Trail

Club Gap 3.8

Buckwheat Knob Trail

477

Twin Falls

Twin Falls Trail

Avery Creek Trail

Clawhammer Road

Bennett Gap 2.3

5.4

Buckhorn Gap Trail

6.1

Maxwell Cove Road

6.2

477

S

Bennett Gap Trail

Horse Stables

N

START/FINISH
Trailhead at southern end of Upper Avery Creek Trail on FS 477, 0.8 miles north of the horseback riding area

TRAIL CONFIGURATION
Loop

SURFACE
Single track • 4.9 miles
Forest road • 2.3 miles

HIGHLIGHTS
Nice views, some pushing required, ruts, log bridges, mud bogs, waterfalls, horse use

TOTAL DISTANCE
7.2 miles

TIME ALLOWANCE
Beginner • 3 hours
Intermediate • 2.25 hrs
Advanced • 1.75 hours

Mileposts

- From start–ride northwest on FS 477 (uphill).
- Mile 2.3–Bennett Gap. Turn right onto Buckwheat Knob Trail (yellow blaze).
- Mile 3.8–after climbing over two very steep knobs, you'll reach Club Gap. Turn right onto Avery Creek Trail (blue blazes).
- Mile 5.4–listen for waterfall off left side of trail.
- Mile 6.1–Buckhorn Gap Trail enters from left.
- Mile 6.2–horse ford and trail splits. Bear right on Upper Avery Creek Trail (yellow blaze).
- Mile 7.2–finish.

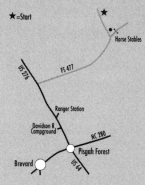

Coontree Gap

Only half of the Coontree Loop is open to bikes. It's got a pretty steep pitch and is better for going down than up. This route takes you up Bennett Gap Trail to the gap and then down Coontree. You'll finish up along US 276, which sees less traffic in the months Coontree is open.

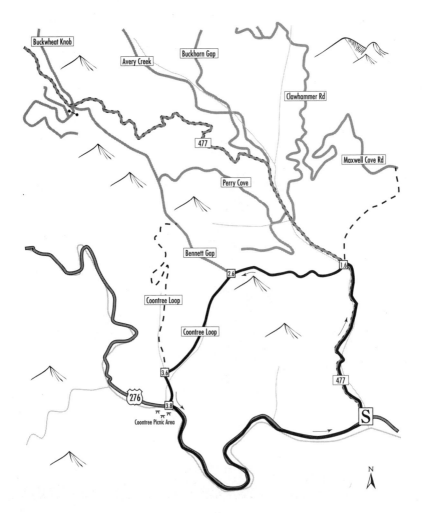

Buckwheat Knob

Avery Creek

Buckhorn Gap

Clawhammer Rd

477

Maxwell Cove Rd

Perry Cove

Bennett Gap

1.6

2.6

Coontree Loop

Coontree Loop

477

3.6

S

276

3.8

Coontree Picnic Area

N

Mileposts

- From start–ride east on FS 477 toward the horse stables.
- Mile 1.6–turn left on Bennett Gap Trail (red blaze). You'll begin climbing immediately.
- Mile 2.6–Coontree Gap and end of climb. Turn left down Coontree Loop Trail (blue blaze).
- Mile 3.6–the hiker only side of the Coontree Loop Trail enters from the right. Continue downhill alongside brook.
- Mile 3.8–Coontree Picnic Area and US 276. Turn left on the highway; watch for passing motorists.
- Mile 6.5–finish.

START/FINISH
Jct. of FS 477 and US 276. Just north of the ranger station.

TRAIL CONFIGURATION
Loop

SURFACE
Single track • 2.2 miles
Forest road • 1.6 miles
Pavement • 2.7 miles

HIGHLIGHTS
Tough uphill, technical downhill, winter views, highway riding

TOTAL DISTANCE
6.5 miles

TIME ALLOWANCE
Beginner • 2.5 hours
Intermediate • 1.75 hrs
Advanced • 1 hours

SEASONAL TRAIL
OPEN OCT 15 – APR 15

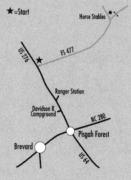

★=Start

Horse Stables

US 276

FS 477

Ranger Station

Davidson R. Campground

NC 280

Pisgah Forest

Brevard

US 64

Coontree Gap

US 276

2000'

1000'

The Pink Beds

This relatively flat area gets its name from the abundance of pink flowering plants. You won't see many flowers during the winter months, but you will enjoy the gently rolling terrain.

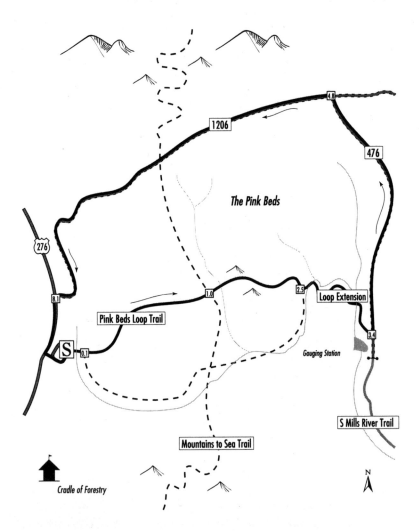

The Pink Beds

1206

476

4.8

276

8.1

Pink Beds Loop Trail

1.0

2.5

Loop Extension

3.4

S

0.1

Gauging Station

S Mills River Trail

Mountains to Sea Trail

Cradle of Forestry

N

START/FINISH
The Pink Beds parking area on US 276

TRAIL CONFIGURATION
Loop

SURFACE
Single track • 4.8 miles
Forest road • 3.3 miles
Pavement • 0.4 miles

HIGHLIGHTS
Views from meadows, rhododendron tunnels, log bridges, rooty trail, South Mills River, interpretive signs

TOTAL DISTANCE
8.5 miles

TIME ALLOWANCE
Beginner • 2.25 hours
Intermediate • 1.5 hours
Advanced • 1 hour

SEASONAL TRAIL
OPEN OCT 15 – APR 15

Mileposts

- From start–ride through gate onto Pink Beds Loop Trail (orange blaze).
- Mile 0.1–take left fork of loop trail. The right fork is closed to bikes.
- Mile 1.0–cross Mountains to Sea Trail (marked by round white dot).
- Mile 2.5–turn left at trail jct. and look for white blazes. This is the Pink Beds Loop Extension. You'll be heading downstream beside the upper South Mills River.
- Mile 3.4–gauging station. Turn left onto FS 476.
- Mile 4.8–turn left onto FS 1206.
- Mile 8.1–turn left onto US 276.
- Mile 8.5–finish.

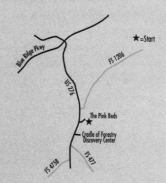

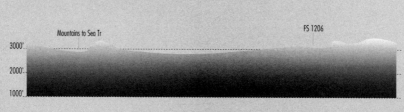

Club Gap

Climbing steeply on single track from the historic Cradle of Forestry, this trail works its way up and over into the popular Avery Creek drainage area. A forest road with a fantastic view of Looking Glass Rock brings you back to the start.

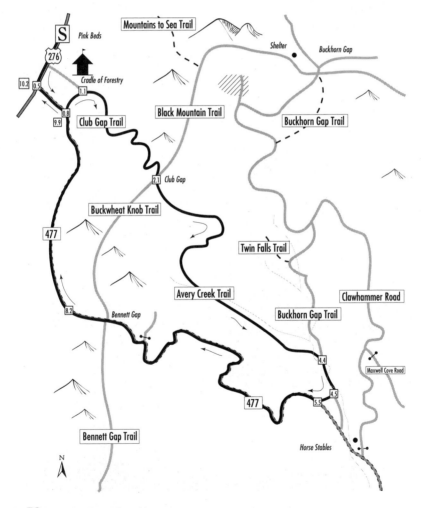

START/FINISH
The Pink Beds parking area on US 276

TRAIL CONFIGURATION
Loop

SURFACE
Single track • 4.6 miles
Forest road • 5.1 miles
Pavement • 1 mile

HIGHLIGHTS
Possible pushing, waterfall, views, log water breaks, the Pink Beds, near Cradle of Forestry

TOTAL DISTANCE
10.7 miles

TIME ALLOWANCE
Beginner • 3 hours
Intermediate • 2 hours
Advanced • 1.5 hours

Mileposts

- From start–ride south on US 276 (left, downhill).
- Mile 0.5–turn left onto FS 477.
- Mile 0.8–take a sharp left on Club Gap Trail (yellow blaze).
- Mile 1.1–turn right off the road bed up Club Gap Trail.
- Mile 2.1–Club Gap. Trails converge here. Continue straight (downhill) on Avery Creek Trail (blue blaze).
- Mile 4.4–Buckhorn Gap Trail enters from left.
- Mile 4.5–horse ford. Turn right onto Upper Avery Trail (yellow blaze).
- Mile 5.5–turn right onto FS 477.
- Mile 8.2–dramatic view of Looking Glass Rock to left.
- Mile 9.9–pass turn onto Club Gap Trail.
- Mile 10.2–turn right onto US 276
- Mile 10.7–finish.

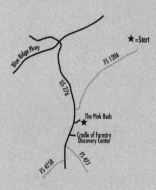

Cradle Loop

*T*he historic Cradle of Forestry is where today's modern forestry practices have their roots, both literally and figuratively. This ride encircles the cradle region, covering much of the same ground where early foresty students learned their science. In the summertime, you can do a variation of this ride by using FS 1206.

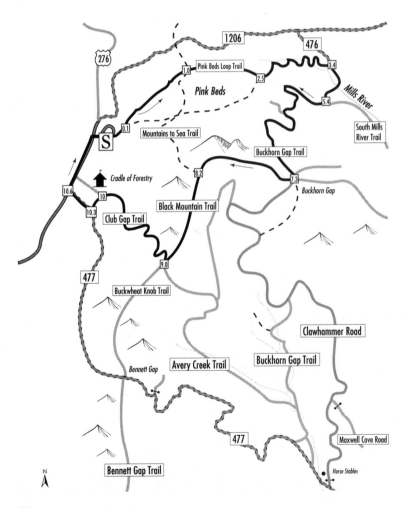

START/FINISH
The Pink Beds parking area on US 276

TRAIL CONFIGURATION
Loop

SURFACE
Single track • 10.3 miles
Forest road • 0.3 miles
Pavement • 0.5 mile

HIGHLIGHTS
Stream crossings, South Mills River, long single track climb, spotty views, fun downhill

TOTAL DISTANCE
11.1 miles

TIME ALLOWANCE
Beginner • 5 hours
Intermediate • 4 hours
Advanced • 2.5 hours

SEASONAL TRAIL
OPEN OCT 15 – APR 15

Mileposts

- From start–ride through gate onto Pink Beds Loop Trail (orange blaze).
- Mile 0.1–take left fork of loop trail. The right fork is closed to bikes.
- Mile 1.0–cross Mountains to Sea Trail (marked by round white dot).
- Mile 2.5–turn left at trail jct. and look for white blazes. This is the Pink Beds Loop Extension. You'll be heading downstream beside the upper South Mills River.
- Mile 3.4–gauging station. Turn right onto FS 476, go around gate and onto South Mills River Trail (white blaze).
- Mile 5.4–turn right up Buckhorn Gap Trail (orange blaze).
- Mile 7.3–turn right up steps onto Black Mountain Trail (white blaze).
- Mile 8.2–Mountains to Sea Trail exits right. Stay on Black Mountain Trail.
- Mile 9–turn right on Club Gap Trail (yellow blaze).
- Mile 10–bear left to stay on Club Gap Trail..
- Mile 10.3–turn right on FS 477.
- Mile 10.6–turn right on US 276.
- Mile 11.1–finish.

4000'

3000'

2000'

Buckhorn Gap   Club Gap

Mountains to Mills River

***A** long mountainous loop, mostly on gravel roads, takes you from the Avery Creek area up and over the ridge to the upper stretches of South Mills River, starting and ending at the Pink Beds.*

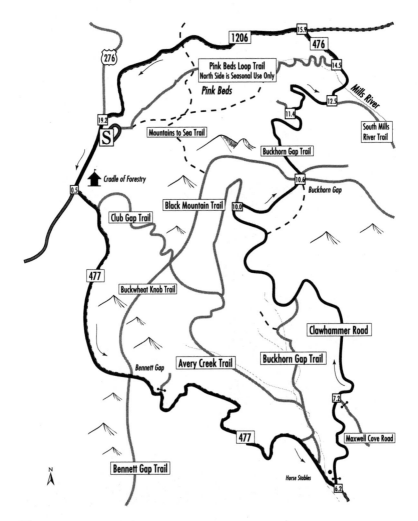

START/FINISH
The Pink Beds parking area on US 276

TRAIL CONFIGURATION
Loop

SURFACE
Single track • 3.1 miles
Double track • 0.8 miles
Forest road • 14.8 miles
Pavement • 0.9 miles

HIGHLIGHTS
Views of Looking Glass Rock and other vistas, horse use, long hills, swimming holes, cascades, timber cuts, old rocky road bed

TOTAL DISTANCE
19.6 miles

TIME ALLOWANCE
Beginner • 5 hours
Intermediate • 3.25 hrs
Advanced • 2.5 hours

Mileposts

- From start—ride south on US 276 (downhill).
- Mile 0.5—turn left onto FS 477.
- Mile 6.2—turn left by horse stables up gated Clawhammer Road.
- Mile 7.2—Maxwell Cove Road enters from right.
- Mile 10—unmarked road enters from left. Bear right.
- Mile 10.6—Buckhorn Gap. Black Mountain/Mountains to Sea and Buckhorn Gap trails cross here and the gravel road forks. Take the left fork down the hill. Buckhorn Gap Trail shares this road bed.
- Mile 11.4—bear right on Buckhorn Gap Trail (orange blaze).
- Mile 12.5—turn left on South Mills River Trail (white blaze).
- Mile 14.5—gauging station. Continue on FS 476.
- Mile 15.9—Turn left onto FS 1206.
- Mile 19.2—turn left onto US 276.
- Mile 19.6—finish.

Squirrel Gap

Heading into one of Pisgah's more remote regions, this is a ride of epic proportions. Allow plenty of time and don't go unprepared (Read: have plenty of food and hydration). You'll follow rivers, climb numerous ridges, and cross a number of streams. And don't expect to see too many others while on the trail.

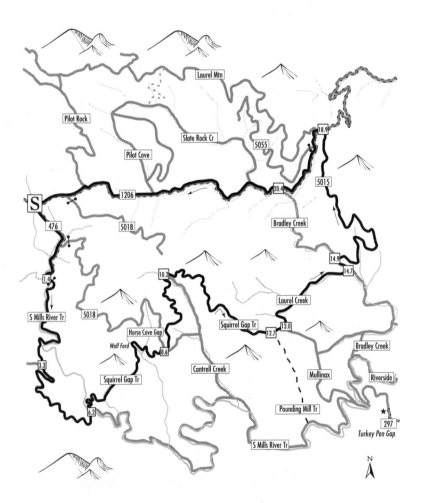

START/FINISH
Go 3.3 miles from
US 276 on FS 1206 and
park at the jct. of
FS 1206 and FS 476

TRAIL CONFIGURATION
Loop

SURFACE
Single track · 13.5 miles
Forest road · 10.9 miles

HIGHLIGHTS
Swinging bridge, S Mills
River, stream crossings,
numerous climbs and
descents, long forest
road uphill

TOTAL DISTANCE
24.4 miles

TIME ALLOWANCE
Beginner · not advised
Intermediate · 6 hours
Advanced · 4.5 hours

Mileposts
- From start–ride south on FS 476.
- Mile 1.4–go around gate and onto South Mills River Trail (white blaze).
- Mile 3.3–top of climb. Buckhorn Gap Trail exits off to the right.
- Mile 6.2–cross South Mills River on a swinging bridge. Bear left onto Squirrel Gap Trail (blue blaze) and begin climb to Squirrel Gap.
- Mile 8.6–Horse Cove Gap Trail crosses. Continue on Squirrel Gap Trail.
- Mile 10.2–Cantrell Creek Trail exits right
- Mile 12.7–Pounding Mill Trail exits right.
- Mile 13–turn left on Laurel Creek Trail (yellow blaze).
- Mile 14.7–cross Bradley Creek and bear left on Bradley Creek Trail.
- Mile 14.9–turn right on FS 5015. It does not look much like a road at this point, but soon will.
- Mile 18.9–after a long, steady climb, turn left on FS 1206.
- Mile 20.4–pass Bradley Creek Trailhead.
- Mile 24.4–finish.

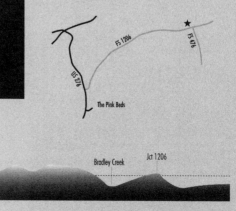

Horse Cove Gap

This ride begins with a forest road climb and views that rival any in Pisgah—just make sure you look over your shoulder on the way up. You'll easily spot Pilot Rock and Slate Rock hanging on the mountainsides below the Blue Ridge Parkway. The single track that follows is as great as the scenery.

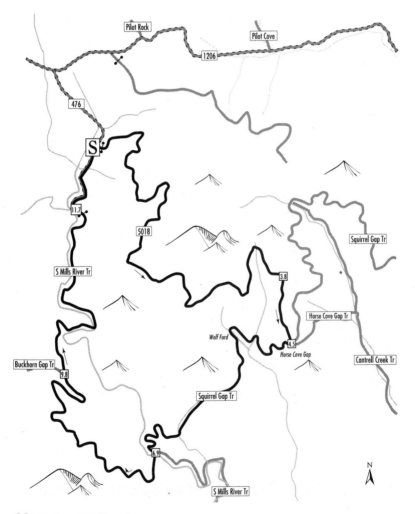

START/FINISH
At gate to FS 5018. Go 3.3 miles from US 276 on FS 1206 and then 1 mile on FS 476

TRAIL CONFIGURATION
Loop

SURFACE
Single track • 7.9 miles
Forest road • 4.3 miles

HIGHLIGHTS
Stunning views, technical single track, swinging bridge, South Mills River, fun downhills

TOTAL DISTANCE
12.2 miles

TIME ALLOWANCE
Beginner • 5 hours
Intermediate • 4 hours
Advanced • 2.5 hours

Mileposts

- From start–go around gate and begin climbing FS 5018.
- Mile 3.8–end of FS 5018. Continue straight onto Horse Cove Gap Trail (red blaze).
- Mile 4.5–turn right on Squirrel Gap Trail (blue blaze)
- Mile 6.9–cross South Mills River on swinging bridge and continue onto South Mills River Trail (white blaze)
- Mile 9.8–climb to where Buckhorn Gap Trail exits left. Bear right, downhill on South Mills River Tr.
- Mile 11.7–go around gate and onto FS 476.
- Mile 12.2–finish.

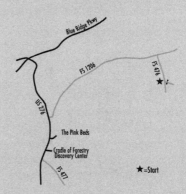

Mills River Area

The eastern side of Pisgah is drained primarily by the North and South Mills Rivers. These two come together to form the Mills River just outside the community of the same name. You'll pass through Mills River en route to any of the rides in this region. This side of Pisgah does not have the so many "attractions" as its western partner. This is perhaps because anything that would fall in to that category is just too hard for the average traveller (read: someone in a car) to get to. If you're willing sweat a lttle, as most any mountain biker is, there is a lot to see and do.

In the North Mills River area you'll find the North Mills River Campground, and most important for mountain bikers, the Trace Ridge Trailhead. This trailhead is the jumping off point for many a mountain bike ride. Here also is the "Never Ending Road" (try riding it to the end and you'll quickly discover how it got its name), and superb trails like Fletcher Creek, Middle Fork, Spencer Branch, and Trace Ridge. There are rides for every ability level, and their popularity can easily be judged by the number of cars in the trailhead parking lot. Don't worry about crowds on the trails, though— there's plenty of room and people spread out quickly.

(continues)

Mills River Area

A long bumpy drive out FS 1206 brings you to a number of small trailheads in the South Mills River area. Don't let the bumpy, dusty drive scare you off, for here you'll find some of the finest rides in all of Pisgah. Demanding routes take you up to where you can ride right across the rock faces of Slate and Pilot Rocks. You'll climb close to 5000 ft. and look out over the entire South Mills River watershed. On the other side of the road, trails take you the length of South Mills River itself. You won't climb so high, but you're bound to get a soaking as you cross and recross the rivers and streams.

Included as well are a couple of rides that originate from the Turkey Pen Gap Trailhead, far on the south end of the river. These rides are well worth the effort, but do note that this area sees more equestrian use than anywhere else in the Pisgah District. So as always, be courteous and follow the rules of the trail.

Slate Rock
Bradley Creek
South Mills Tour
Laurel Mountain
Big Creek
Middle Fork
Fletcher Creek
Spencer Branch
Trace Ridge
Spencer Gap
Wash Creek
Bear Branch
Old Cantrell Creek Lodge
Riverside

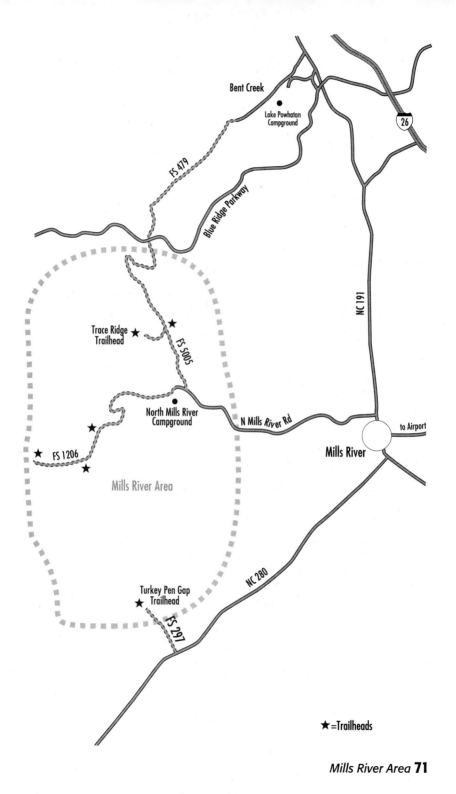

Bent Creek

Lake Powhatan
Campground

26

FS 479

Blue Ridge Parkway

NC 191

Trace Ridge
Trailhead ★

★

FS 5005

★

North Mills River
Campground

N Mills River Rd

to Airport

★ FS 1206

★

Mills River Area

Mills River

NC 280

Turkey Pen Gap
Trailhead ★

FS 297

★ =Trailheads

Slate Rock

*T*his Slate Rock is a large stone outcropping which hangs above Pilot Cove at just over 3600 feet. This short ride takes you to the top of the rock for the view and then immediately back down. It's steep going up and very steep coming down. At the top, you'll ride on bare rock and get an astounding view.

Great views on Slate Rock

To Laurel MTN Trail

Waterfall

1.5

Pilot Cove/Slate Rock Creek Tr

Slate Rock

2.4

Pilot Cove Loop

Pilot Cove

Pilot Cove/Slate Rock Creek Tr

Waterfall

Beaver Bog

3.7 0.2

S

1206

N

START/FINISH

There are two trailheads for the Pilot Cove/Slate Rock Creek Trail. Start at the one farthest west on FS 1206, 6.8 miles from North Mills River Campground

TRAIL CONFIGURATION

Loop

SURFACE

Single track • 3.9 miles

HIGHLIGHTS

Quiet fern-filled cove, beaver bog, may have to push on ascent, bare rock riding, great view, very steep descent

TOTAL DISTANCE

3.9 miles

TIME ALLOWANCE

Beginner • 2 hours (but most of it may be walking with the bike)
Intermediate • 1.5 hours
Advanced • 1 hour

Mileposts

- From start–ride up Pilot Cove/Slate Rock Creek Trail (blue blaze)
- Mile 0.2–bear left to continue on Pilot Cove/Slate Rock Creek Trail. Be aware that at times parts of this trail are covered by a beaver swamp.
- Mile 1.5–gain the ridge. Turn right on the Pilot Cove Loop Trail (yellow blaze) and continue to climb.
- Mile 2.4–ride out onto Slate Rock. Be careful and don't get too close to the edge. Get ready for a very steep downhill.
- Mile 3.7–bottom of hill. Turn left on Pilot Cove/Slate Rock Creek Trail.
- Mile 3.9–finish.

Mile 1.5   Slate Rock

4000'
3000'
2000'

Pilot Cove/Slate Rock Creek

This ride takes you up Slate Rock Creek and past two waterfalls before making a steep jump up onto Slate Rock itself. Slate Rock is a large outcropping of stone hanging above Pilot Cove. Take in the fantastic view and then take the plunge down into Pilot Cove.

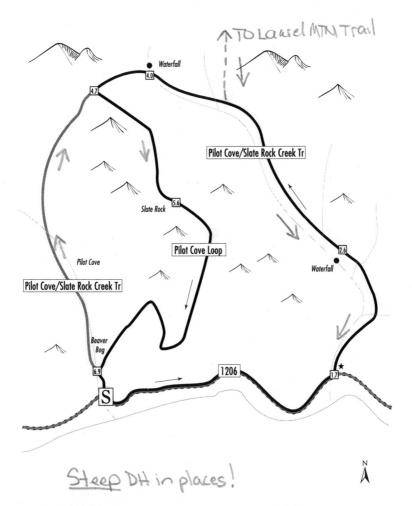

TO Laurel MTN Trail

Waterfall

4.0

4.7

Pilot Cove/Slate Rock Creek Tr

5.6

Slate Rock

Pilot Cove Loop

2.6

Pilot Cove

Waterfall

Pilot Cove/Slate Rock Creek Tr

Beaver Bog

6.9

1206

1.7

S

Steep DH in places!

N

START/FINISH
There are two trailheads for the Pilot Cove/Slate Rock Creek Trail. Start at the one farthest west on FS 1206, 6.8 miles from North Mills River Campground

TRAIL CONFIGURATION
Loop

SURFACE
Single track • 5.4 miles
Forest road • 1.7 miles

HIGHLIGHTS
Log bridges, fern glens, steep section, clifftop view, bare rock riding, waterfalls, mud bogs, very steep downhill

TOTAL DISTANCE
7.1 miles

TIME ALLOWANCE
Beginner • 3.5 hours
Intermediate • 2.5 hours
Advanced • 1.5 hours

Mileposts

- From start–ride east on FS 1206 (downhill).
- Mile 1.7–turn left onto Pilot Cove/ Slate Rock Creek Trail (blue blaze).
- Mile 2.6–there is a waterfall off the left side of the trail. You can hear it before you see it.
- Mile 4.0–a steady climb will bring you to another waterfall. This one is on the right.
- Mile 4.7–gain Slate Rock Ridge. Turn left here and climb up some more on the Pilot Cove Loop Trail.
- Mile 5.6–Slate Rock. The views here are fantastic–just don't get too close to the edge. A very steep downhill section is coming up soon.
- Mile 6.9–bottom out in Pilot Cove. Turn left.
- Mile 7.1–finish.

Bradley Creek

If you don't mind getting your feet wet, you'll love this ride. There are no fewer than twelve stream crossings. Don't worry—the ride on the gravel road back to the start will give your shoes plenty of time to dry out. Avoid this ride in cold weather.

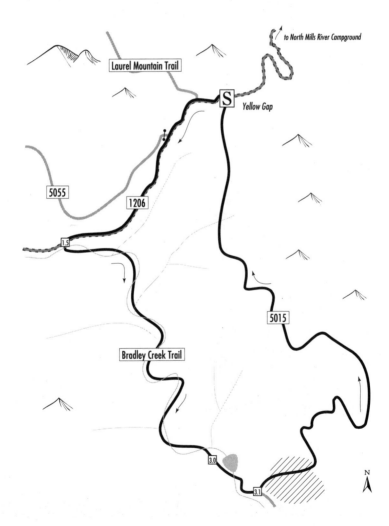

to North Mills River Campground

Laurel Mountain Trail

S

Yellow Gap

5055

1206

1.5

Bradley Creek Trail

5015

3.0

3.1

N

START/FINISH
Gate to FS 5015. This is 3.3 miles west of North Mills River Campground on FS 1206

TRAIL CONFIGURATION
Loop

SURFACE
Single track • 1.6 miles
Forest road • 5.4 miles

HIGHLIGHTS
Numerous stream crossings, mud bogs, timber cuts, views, cascades, bluff

TOTAL DISTANCE
7 miles

TIME ALLOWANCE
Beginner • 2.5 hours
Intermediate • 1.75 hrs
Advanced • 1.25 hours

Mileposts

- From start—ride west on FS 1206 to the bottom of the hill.
- Mile 1.5—turn left onto Bradley Creek Trail (orange blaze). This trail starts at the first pull-out on the left at the bottom of the hill. The trail sign is on the far side of the creek. You immediately cross the creek and turn left downstream.
- Mile 3.0—bluff beside dam and small reservoir.
- Mile 3.1—enter timber cut and turn left (uphill) onto unmarked FS 5015. You'll ride through many timber cuts as you gradually climb the ridge back to the start.
- Mile 7.0—finish.

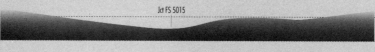

South Mills Tour

This is most definitely a warm weather ride and one you will not soon forget. Allow plenty of time. The multiple stream and river crossings take their toll and you will get wet, but the ride is guaranteed to keep you cool on a hot summer day!

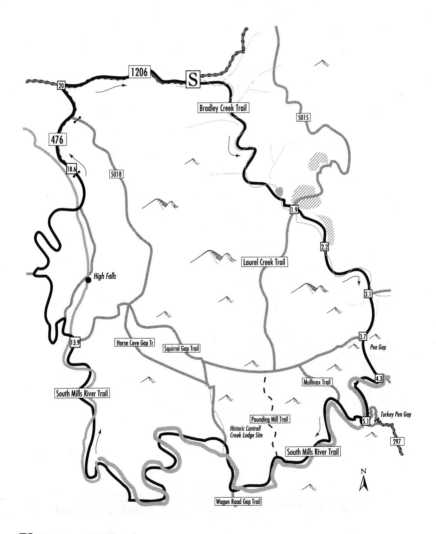

START/FINISH

Bradley Creek Trailhead, 4.8 miles west of North Mills River Campground on FS 1206. It's the first pullout on the left at the bottom of the hill past FS 5015. The trail sign is on the other side of the creek.

TRAIL CONFIGURATION

Loop

SURFACE

Single track • 18.6 miles
Forest road • 5.3 miles

HIGHLIGHTS

Numerous stream and river crossings, rocky sections, horse use, mud bogs, swinging bridges, few hills, historic lodge site

TOTAL DISTANCE

23.9 miles

TIME ALLOWANCE

Beginner • not advised
Intermediate • 5 hours
Advanced • 4 hours

Mileposts

- From start–cross creek and ride downstream on the Bradley Creek Trail (orange blazes).
- Mile 1.9–FS 5015 enters left, then Laurel Creek Trail right.
- Mile 2.2–at end of last big field, cross creek to right.
- Mile 3.1–take right fork and begin heading uphill.
- Mile 3.7–Squirrel Gap Trail enters on right. Bear left.
- Mile 4.3–Riverside Trail enters from left. Bear right.
- Mile 5.1–4-way trails jct. Turn right and cross river on South Mills River Trail (white blazes). You'll follow this trail for the next 13.5 miles with many river crossings.
- Mile 13.9–Squirrel Gap Trail enters on right. Cross bridge. A little bit farther on, the trail turns sharply back to the left.. Continue to follow the white blazes.
- Mile 18.6–trail ends and FS 476 begins.
- Mile 20.0–turn right onto FS 1206.
- Mile 23.9–finish.

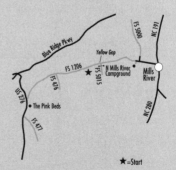

★ =Start

Laurel Mountain

*T*his ride starts out with one of the best single track climbs in Pisgah; all but the last (steep!) half-mile to the top is pure joy. Well-honed technical skills make getting back down a treat in itself. You'll zig and zag through many a rocky switchback and over more humps than you can count before returning to the forest road below.

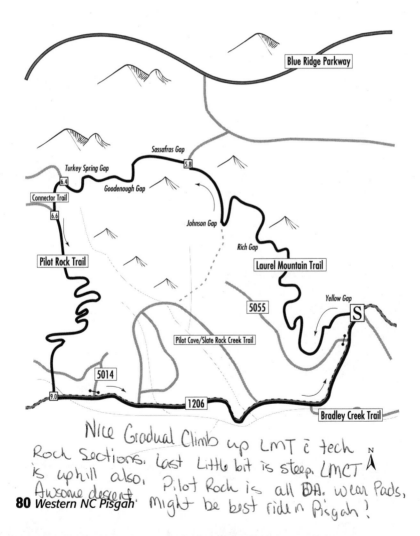

Nice Gradual Climb up LMT c̄ tech
Rock Sections. Last Little bit is steep. LMCT
is uphill also. Pilot Rock is all BA. Wear Pads,
Awsome descent. might be best ridein Pisgah!

5/30/08

START/FINISH
Laurel Mountain Trailhead, located 3.5 miles west of North Mills River Campground on FS 1206.

TRAIL CONFIGURATION
Loop

SURFACE
Single track • 9.1 miles
Forest road • 4.4 miles

HIGHLIGHTS
Gradual climb, rhododendron and laurel tunnels, one very steep uphill pitch, small boulder fields, rocky switchbacks, numerous whoops

TOTAL DISTANCE
13.5 miles

TIME ALLOWANCE
Beginner • not advised
Intermediate • 3 hours
Advanced • 2 hours

Mileposts

- From start–ride uphill on Laurel Mountain Trail (blue blazes)
- Mile 5.8–Sassafras Gap. An unmarked trail exits to the right. Bear left to start up a very steep climb.
- Mile 6.4–Turkey Spring Gap. Turn left onto Laurel Mountain Connector Trail (yellow blazes).
- Mile 6.6–turn left onto Pilot Rock Trail (orange blazes). The next 2.5 miles are all downhill, with technical, rocky switchbacks.
- Mile 9–you'll cross an old skid road, then a creek, and then turn left onto FS 1206.
- Mile 13.5–finish.

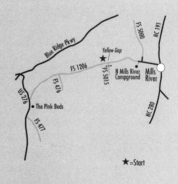

★ =Start

Sassafras Gap Turkey Spring Gap

FS 1206

4000'
3000'
2000'

Big Creek

This is a very arduous ride going from 2600 ft. to 4100 ft. That's the first 13 miles. Hang on, you'll drop from Sassafras Gap to Big Creek in no time, losing that same 1500 ft. in just over a mile! The views are great and the creek is beautiful and cool—and wet.

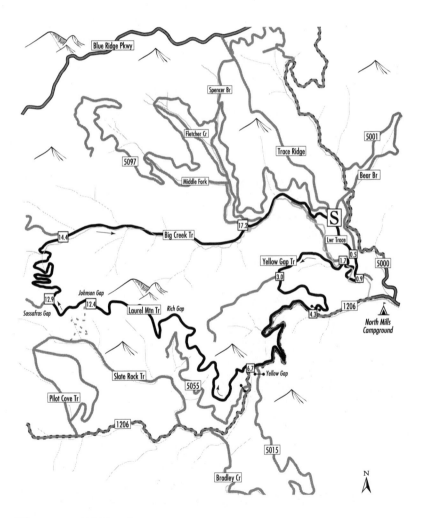

START/FINISH
To get to the trailhead, drive north for 2 miles on FS 5000 from North Mills River Campground and then turn left on FS 142 for 0.5 miles

TRAIL CONFIGURATION
Loop

SURFACE
Single track • 15.1 miles
Forest road • 3.7 miles

HIGHLIGHTS
big and numerous stream crossings, long steady climb on road and trail, several steep uphills, very, very steep downhill, views

TOTAL DISTANCE
18.8 miles

TIME ALLOWANCE
Beginner • not advised
Intermediate • 5 hours
Advanced • 3.5 hours

Mileposts

- From start–ride past info board onto Lower Trace Ridge Trail (orange blaze).
- Mile 0.5–Wash Creek Trail exits on the left. Continue on Lower Trace.
- Mile 0.9–turn left on North Mills River Trail (blue blaze). You'll cross the river several times.
- Mile 1.7–turn left up Yellow Gap Trail (blue blaze). It is steep and washed out for a short ways.
- Mile 3.0–turn left on forest road.
- Mile 4.3–bottom of hill. Turn right. on FS 1206. Begin long climb.
- Mile 6.7–turn right on Laurel Mountain Trail (blue blaze)
- Mile 12.4–Johnson Gap. An unnamed trail turns off left here.
- Mile 12.9–Sassafras Gap and end of climbing. Turn right on un-marked trail to begin steep descent.
- Mile 14.4–bear right on Big Creek Trail (yellow blaze).
- Mile 17.2–Hendersonville Reser-voir. Continue onto Hendersonville Reservoir Road.
- Mile 18.8–finish.

Middle Fork

After you take in the views from what is known as the "Never Ending Road," you'll dip down through fern-filled woods, small meadows and alongside a small cascading stream. This one is a real beauty.

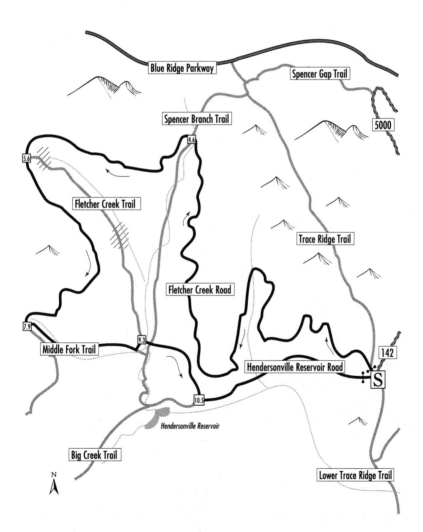

Blue Ridge Parkway

Spencer Gap Trail

Spencer Branch Trail
4.6

5000

5.6

Fletcher Creek Trail

Trace Ridge Trail

Fletcher Creek Road

7.9

Middle Fork Trail
9.3

142

Hendersonville Reservoir Road
S

10.5

Hendersonville Reservoir

Big Creek Trail

Lower Trace Ridge Trail

N

Mileposts

- From start–ride through gate and out Fletcher Creek Road.
- Mile 4.6–cross Spencer Branch Trail.
- Mile 5.6–Fletcher Creek Trail enters on left.
- Mile 7.9–turn left onto Middle Fork Trail (orange blaze).
- Mile 9.3–turn right onto Fletcher Creek Trail (blue blaze), cross creek and then cross Spencer Branch Trail.
- Mile 10.5–turn left onto Hendersonville Reservoir Road.
- Mile 11.8–finish.

START/FINISH
To get to the trailhead, drive north for 2 miles on FS 5000 from North Mills River Campground and then turn left on FS 142 for 0.5 miles

TRAIL CONFIGURATION
Loop

SURFACE
Single track • 2.6 miles
Forest road • 9.2 miles

HIGHLIGHTS
Gravel road, views, stream crossings, mud bogs, meadows, open woods, horse use, cascades

TOTAL DISTANCE
11.8 miles

TIME ALLOWANCE
Beginner • 3 hours
Intermediate • 2 hours
Advanced • 1.25 hours

Bent Creek

Blue Ridge Pkwy

FS 142   FS 5000   NC 191

FS 1206

N Mills River Campground   Mills River

NC 280

★=Start

Jct Middle Fork Tr   Cross Fletcher Cr

2000'

1000'

Fletcher Creek

*T*his is a great ride for all ability levels. Starting on what is known to locals as the "Never Ending Road," you'll ride out to the headwaters of Fletcher Creek and then you and the stream will build up steam together as you return on a beautiful trail.

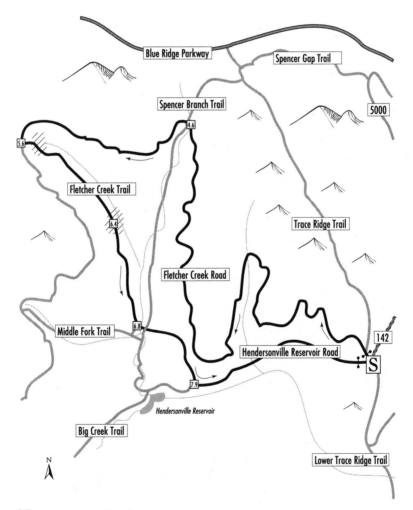

Blue Ridge Parkway

Spencer Gap Trail

Spencer Branch Trail

4.6

5000

5.6

Fletcher Creek Trail

6.4

Trace Ridge Trail

Fletcher Creek Road

Middle Fork Trail   6.8

142

Hendersonville Reservoir Road   S

7.9

Hendersonville Reservoir

Big Creek Trail

N

Lower Trace Ridge Trail

START/FINISH
To get to the trailhead, drive north for 2 miles on FS 5000 from North Mills River Campground and then turn left on FS 142 for 0.5 miles

TRAIL CONFIGURATION
Loop

SURFACE
Single track • 2.3 miles
Forest road • 6.8 miles

HIGHLIGHTS
Gravel road cruising, few small hills, creek crossing, open woods, meadows, horse use

TOTAL DISTANCE
9.1 miles

TIME ALLOWANCE
Beginner • 2 hours
Intermediate • 1.5 hours
Advanced • 1 hour

Mileposts

- From start–ride through gate and out Fletcher Creek Road.
- Mile 4.6–Spencer Branch Trail crosses road.
- Mile 5.6–turn left onto Fletcher Creek Trail (blue blaze.)
- Mile 6.4–trail crosses big meadow.
- Mile 6.8–Middle Fork Trail enters from right. Cross Fletcher Creek and intersect Spencer Branch Trail. Continue straight on Fletcher Creek Trail.
- Mile 7.9–turn left on Hendersonville Reservoir Road.
- Mile 9.1–finish.

Bent Creek

Blue Ridge Pkwy

FS 142 FS 5000 NC 191

FS 1206

N Mills River Campground Mills River

★=Start

NC 280

Jct Fletcher Cr Trail

Cross Fletcher Cr

2000'

1000'

Spencer Branch

*W*ith relatively few hills, this ride is jazzed up by some rather technical creek crossings and narrow hillside trails. Expect to get muddy on this one, especially after wet weather.

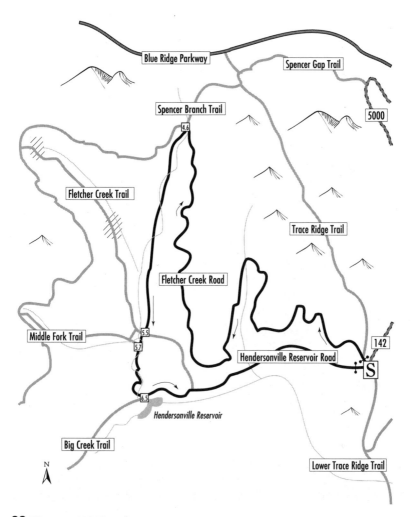

Blue Ridge Parkway

Spencer Gap Trail

Spencer Branch Trail

4.6

5000

Fletcher Creek Trail

Trace Ridge Trail

Fletcher Creek Road

Middle Fork Trail

5.5

5.7

142

Hendersonville Reservoir Road

S

6.5

Hendersonville Reservoir

Big Creek Trail

N

Lower Trace Ridge Trail

START/FINISH
To get to the trailhead, drive north for 2 miles on FS 5000 from North Mills River Campground and then turn left on FS 142 for 0.5 miles.

TRAIL CONFIGURATION
Loop

SURFACE
Single track • 6.2 miles
Forest road • 1.9 miles

HIGHLIGHTS
Some technical riding, mud bogs, creek crossings, horse use

TOTAL DISTANCE
8.1 miles

TIME ALLOWANCE
Beginner • 2 hours
Intermediate • 1.5 hours
Advanced • 1 hour

Mileposts

- From start–ride through gate and out Fletcher Creek Road.
- Mile 4.6–turn left onto Spencer Branch Trail (orange blaze).
- Mile 5.5–cross Fletcher Creek Trail.
- Mile 5.7–Middle Fork Trail enters. on right. Stay on Spencer Branch Trail.
- Mile 6.5–Hendersonville Reservoir. Big Creek Trail enters on right. Spencer Branch Trail ends and Hendersonville Reservoir Road begins. Continue on Hendersonville Reservoir Road.
- Mile 8.1–finish.

Jct Spencer Br Tr

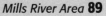

2000'
1000'

Trace Ridge

*A*though this route is not extreme, it is the most difficult trail in the popular Fletcher Creek area. You'll climb steadily and sometimes steeply for most of the first two miles before quickly descending to cross Fletcher Creek Road. The return is along Spencer Branch Trail.

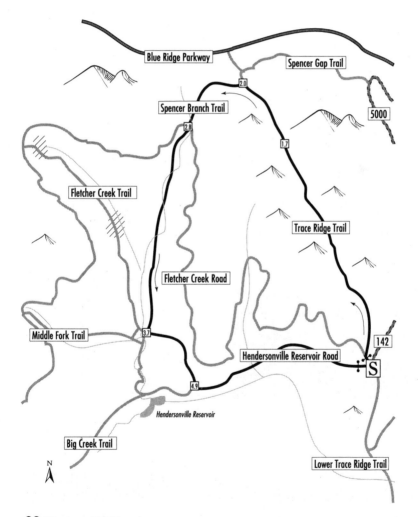

Blue Ridge Parkway

Spencer Gap Trail

2.0

Spencer Branch Trail

2.8

1.7

5000

Fletcher Creek Trail

Trace Ridge Trail

Fletcher Creek Road

Middle Fork Trail

3.7

142

Hendersonville Reservoir Road

S

4.9

Hendersonville Reservoir

N

Big Creek Trail

Lower Trace Ridge Trail

START/FINISH
To get to the trailhead, drive north for 2 miles on FS 5000 from North Mills River Campground and then turn left on FS 142 for 0.5 miles

TRAIL CONFIGURATION
Loop

SURFACE
Single track • 4.9 miles
Forest road • 1.2 miles

HIGHLIGHTS
Long rocky climb, ridge riding, spotty views, timber cuts, steep downhill, horse use

TOTAL DISTANCE
6.1 miles

TIME ALLOWANCE
Beginner • 2.5 hours
Intermediate • 1.75 hrs
Advanced • 1 hour

Mileposts

- From start–ride through gate onto Fletcher Creek Road and then immediately take a right up over whoop-te-doos onto Trace Ridge Trail (orange blazes).
- Mile 1.7–top of ridge.
- Mile 2.0–turn left down Spencer Branch Trail (yellow blazes). This is very steep.
- Mile 2.8–cross Fletcher Creek Road to continue on Spencer Branch Trail.
- Mile 3.7–turn left on Fletcher Creek Trail (blue blaze).
- Mile 4.9–turn left on Hendersonville Reservoir Road.
- Mile 6.1–finish.

Bent Creek

Blue Ridge Pkwy

FS 142 FS 5000 NC 191

FS 1206

N Mills River Campground Mills River

NC 280

★ =Start

Trace Ridge

Jct Fletcher Cr Tr

3000'
2000'
1000'

Spencer Gap

Taking advantage of gravel roads for most of the climbing, this ride takes you out and up to a ridge just below the Blue Ridge Parkway. You'll return on the technical single track of the Spencer Branch Trail.

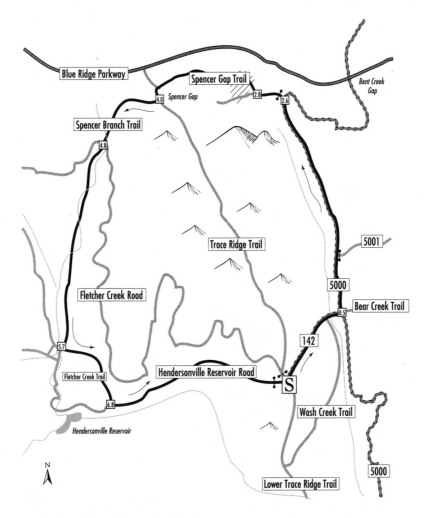

Blue Ridge Parkway

Spencer Gap Trail

4.0 Spencer Gap

2.8

2.6

Bent Creek Gap

Spencer Branch Trail

4.8

Trace Ridge Trail

5001

5000

Fletcher Creek Road

Bear Creek Trail

0.5

142

5.7

Fletcher Creek Trail

Hendersonville Reservoir Road

S

6.8

Wash Creek Trail

Hendersonville Reservoir

N

5000

Lower Trace Ridge Trail

START/FINISH

To get to the trailhead, drive north for 2 miles on FS 5000 from North Mills River Campground and then turn left on FS 142 for 0.5 miles

TRAIL CONFIGURATION

Loop

SURFACE

Single track • 4.2 miles
Forest road • 3.8 miles

HIGHLIGHTS

Creek crossings, mud bogs, spotty views, short steep climbs, short steep technical down-hill, horse use

TOTAL DISTANCE

8 miles

TIME ALLOWANCE

Beginner • 3 hours
Intermediate • 2.25 hrs
Advanced • 1.5 hours

Mileposts

- From start–ride towards FS 5000 on FS 142.
- Mile 0.5–turn left onto FS 5000.
- Mile 2.6–turn left onto Spencer Gap Trail. This is marked by a gate on the left in a sharp right bend in the road. The trail sign is 100 feet up the trail (yellow blaze).
- Mile 2.8–trail forks just before a field. Take the right fork up the hill and through the field.
- Mile 4.0–Spencer Gap. Turn left onto Trace Ridge Trail and then immediately right down Spencer Branch Trail (yellow blaze).
- Mile 4.8–cross Fletcher Creek Road.
- Mile 5.7–turn left on Fletcher Creek Trail (blue blaze).
- Mile 6.8–turn left on Hendersonville Reservoir Road.
- Mile 8.0–finish.

Spencer Gap

Jct Fletcher Cr Tr

3000'

2000'

1000'

Wash Creek

***A** great ride for the beginner who wants a try at single track riding. It's short and all the single track is downhill. This is also a nice addition to any of the other rides in the Fletcher Creek area.*

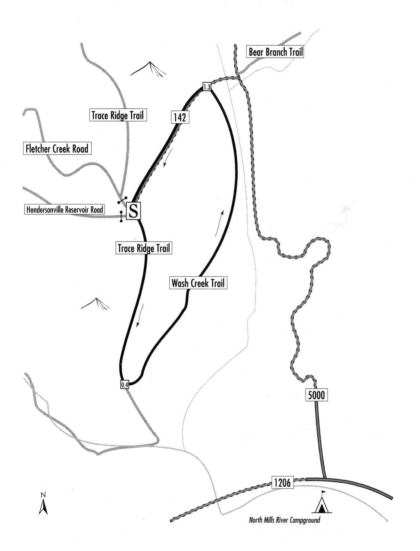

Mileposts

- From start–ride downhill on Trace Ridge Trail (orange blazes). The trail is just past the information station.
- Mile 0.4–turn sharply back to left on Wash Creek Trail (yellow blazes). It's easy to miss this turn, so be on the lookout as you are careening down the hill.
- Mile 1.3–turn left on FS 142.
- Mile 1.8–finish.

START/FINISH
To get to the trailhead, drive north for 2 miles on FS 5000 from North Mills River Campground and then turn left on FS 142 for 0.5 miles

TRAIL CONFIGURATION
Loop

SURFACE
Single track • 1.3 miles
Forest road • 0.5 miles

HIGHLIGHTS
Short, the single track is all downhill, horse use

TOTAL DISTANCE
1.8 miles

TIME ALLOWANCE
Beginner • 30 minutes
Intermediate • 20 min
Advanced • 15 minutes

★ =Start

Jct Wash Cr Tr

Wash Creek

Up FS 142

2000'

1000'

Bear Branch

A*s you meander through a somewhat confusing network of trails, you'll notice that blue-blazed trails seem to head off in all directions. This is the best and easiest route through that maze. The return along Bear Branch is delightful.*

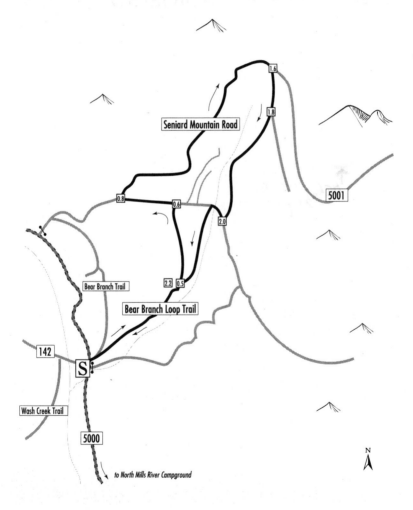

START/FINISH
2 miles north on FS 5000 from North Mills River Campground, just across from FS 142.

TRAIL CONFIGURATION
Loop w/ extension

SURFACE
Single track • 2.1 miles
Forest road • 0.8 miles

HIGHLIGHTS
Horse use, hidden turns, blazed and unblazed trail network, small streams, rocky in places

TOTAL DISTANCE
2.9 miles

TIME ALLOWANCE
Beginner • 1 hour
Intermediate • 45 min
Advanced • 20 minutes

Mileposts

- From start–ride over whoop-te-doos just to left of gate onto Bear Branch Loop Trail (blue blaze). The steep, seldom used Bear Branch Trail exits immediately to the left.
- Mile 0.5–bear left at fork to begin the loop.
- Mile 0.6–turn left onto woods road.
- Mile 0.8–turn right onto Seniard Mountain Road.
- Mile 1.6–turn right onto Bear Branch Loop Trail.
- Mile 1.8–trail forks. Bear right down the hill.
- Mile 2.0–turn right on blue-blazed woods road and then immediately left on trail after crossing bridge.
- Mile 2.2–bear left as you close the loop.
- Mile 2.9–finish.

★ =Start

Jct Bear Br Loop

2000'
1000'

Old Cantrell Creek Lodge

***E**asy, with a few hills and several suspension bridge river crossings, this ride takes you up the South Mills River to an old lodge chimney. Built in 1890, the historic lodge itself was moved in 1970 to its present location at the Cradle of Forestry.*

Wide Track. Easy Ride.   Rode as 1st Leg of Loop.

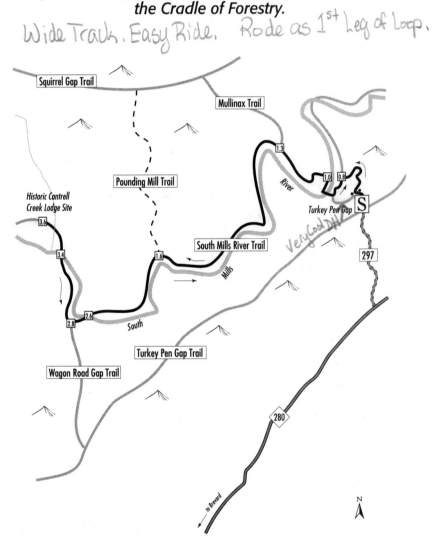

START/FINISH
Turkey Pen Gap Trailhead at northern end of FS 297. FS 297 is located off NC 280, 5 miles east of the NC 280/US 276 jct. in Pisgah Forest.

TRAIL CONFIGURATION
Out-and-Back

SURFACE
Single track • 7.2 miles

HIGHLIGHTS
Suspension bridges, historic site, heavy horse use, swimming holes, wide trail

TOTAL DISTANCE
7.2 miles

TIME ALLOWANCE
Beginner • 2 hours
Intermediate • 1.5 hours
Advanced • 1 hour

Mileposts

- From start–ride through gate and down roadbed to right on South Mills River Trail.
- Mile 0.8–4-way trails jct. Turn left and ride 0.1 mile upstream and cross river on swinging bridge.
- Mile 1.0–turn left up the hill on South Mills River Trail (white blaze).
- Mile 1.3–Mullinax Trail enters on right.
- Mile 1.6–Pounding Mill Trail enters on right.
- Mile 2.6–cross river on swinging bridge.
- Mile 2.8–Wagon Road Gap Trail enters from left.
- Mile 3.4–cross river on swinging bridge.
- Mile 3.6–site of Cantrell Creek Lodge. There is a historical sign by the old chimney. Turn around here.
- Mile 7.2–finish

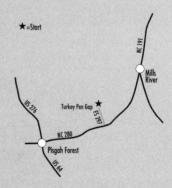

Riverside

With 10 stream and river crossings, you're certain not to get overheated, and except for the short climb over Pea Gap, you never leave the water's edge. Steer clear of this ride altogether in cold weather. There are some deep sand sections that will get your attention and beware of some slippery, bumpy roots as well. All that said, this can be a really nice ride.

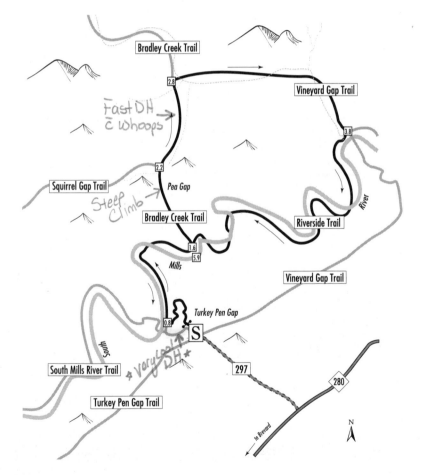

START/FINISH
Turkey Pen Gap Trailhead at northern end of FS 297. FS 297 is located off NC 280, 5 miles east of the NC 280/US 276 jct. in Pisgah Forest.

TRAIL CONFIGURATION
Loop w/extension

SURFACE
Single track • 7.8 miles

HIGHLIGHTS
River crossings (some are waist deep), heavy horse use, sand and mud bogs, exposed roots

TOTAL DISTANCE
7.8 miles

TIME ALLOWANCE
Beginner • 2.5 hours
Intermediate • 1.75 hrs
Advanced • 1.25 hours

Mileposts

- From start–ride down the gated road located to the right of the South Mills River Trail.
- Mile 0.8–at river, turn sharply to the right onto the Bradley Creek Trail (orange blaze).
- Mile 1.6–Riverside Trail enters from the right. Bear left (uphill) on Bradley Creek Trail (orange blaze).
- Mile 2.2–Squirrel Gap Trail enters from the left.
- Mile 2.8–trail forks 100 feet after crossing a small stream. Take the right fork across Bradley Creek onto Vineyard Gap Trail (yellow blaze).
- Mile 3.8–turn right onto Riverside Trail (blue blaze), cross Bradley Creek and ride beside South Mills River.
- Mile 5.9–bear left onto Bradley Creek Trail (orange blaze) and finish the ride by returning the way you came.
- Mile 7.8–finish.

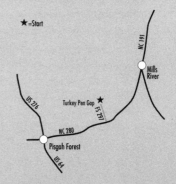

Pea Gap

2000'
1000'

Westside Pisgah Area

On Pisgah's westside you'll find the highest elevations in the region. Here the Blue Ridge Parkway snakes and curves its way to Richland-Balsam, the highest point of the entire Parkway at 6410 feet. Along the way it passes through Graveyard Fields and by the Devil's Courthouse. Much of the area is designated wilderness. There are actually two areas, Shining Rock Wilderness and Middle Prong Wilderness, seperated by NC Highway 215. These areas are very remote, wild and off limits to bicycles. Still, if you really do want to get off the beaten track, these are great places to take a hike and a break from your bike.

The south side of the Parkway is home to the very headwaters of the French Broad River. It's hard to believe that the tiny streams trickling down the sides of the mountains can in such a short time become the mighty river that flows through Asheville, which as the crow flys is not too far away.

Trails for cyclists in this region are not so numerous as in those areas to the east, yet the trails are there and they should be ridden. This section has the two highest-altitude routes available in this book. In fact, they are the highest of any in the entire Off The Beaten Track mountain bike guide series. Both the Flat Laurel Creek ride and the Ivestor Gap ride originate from the Black Balsam Trailhead, which lies just under the 6000-ft. mark.

(continues)

Westside Pisgah Area

This area is very popular in the warmer months because it's cool, so expect to see lots of folks on nice summer weekend days. In late August when the blueberries are ripe, expect to see even more. At other times and during the week, you're likely to have it all to yourself. It is no wonder people flock here; the scenery is magnificient. A virtually treeless vista opens up extensive views, and when the weather is right, banks of mist roll through a landscape reminisent of the Scottish Highlands.

Down below the Devil's Courthouse I've included a couple of more rides. One circles around the upper edges of Pilot Mountain and the other explores Summey Cove and Courthouse Falls. Flanking the ridges in this area are numerous logging roads, so if you're up for exploring, there's good potential for even more. But unlike the rides mentioned above, expect to see few if any people in this area.

Pilot Mountain
Summey Cove
Flat Laurel Creek
Ivestor Gap

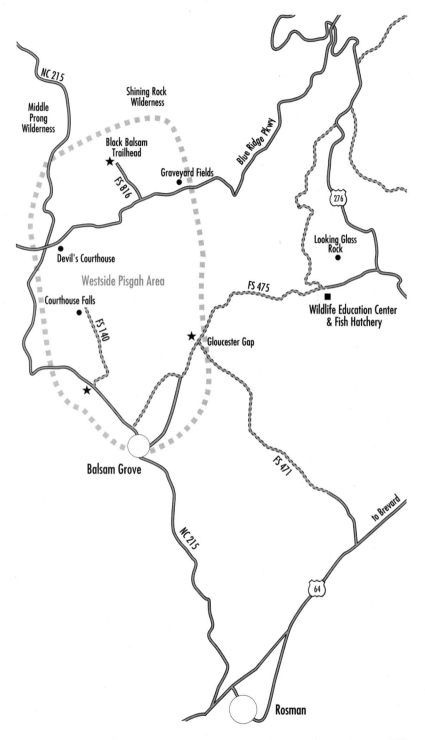

Pilot Mountain

Igh-altitude trails at their best, with spectacular views of John, Cedar, and Looking Glass Rocks. You'll circle the top of Pilot Mountain. Watch for the hidden turn just past Farlow Gap. If you miss it, this really will be a long, long ride!

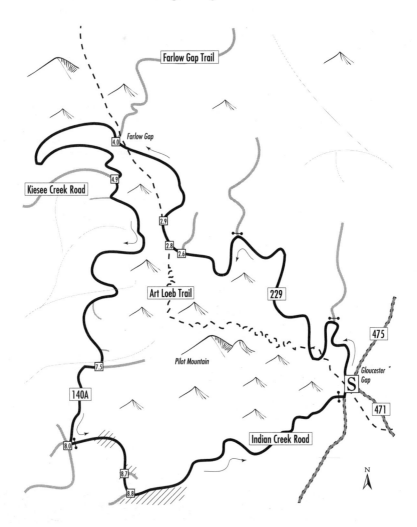

Farlow Gap Trail

Farlow Gap
4.0

4.9

Kiesee Creek Road

2.9

2.8
2.6

Art Loeb Trail

229

475

7.5

Pilot Mountain

Gloucester Gap
S

140A

471

8.0

Indian Creek Road

8.7

8.8

N

START/FINISH
Gloucester Gap, 5 miles west of Fish Hatchery on FS 475. FS 229, 471, and 475 all meet here.

TRAIL CONFIGURATION
Loop

SURFACE
Single track • 8.5 miles
Forest road • 2.6 miles

HIGHLIGHTS
Great views, long climbs, very rocky trail sections, whoop-te-doos, cascades, at least one hidden turn

TOTAL DISTANCE
11.1 miles

TIME ALLOWANCE
Beginner • 4+ hours
Intermediate • 3 hours
Advanced • 2 hours

Mileposts

- From start–ride up FS 229.
- Mile 2.6–road forks, with dirt barriers on each fork. Take the upper (left) fork up the old rocky road bed.
- Mile 2.8–Art Loeb/Mountains to Sea Trail enters left.
- Mile 2.9–Art Loeb/Mountains to Sea Trail exits left.
- Mile 4.0–Farlow Gap. Trails jct. Continue on old road.
- Mile 4.9–just after the old, washed-out roadbed you are on turns into a newer, seeded road bed, the trail will make two big switchbacks. In the middle of the second one a hidden trail turns off to the left. It's marked by a small dirt barricade. Turn left here.
- Mile 7.5–unmarked trail enters from the left.
- Mile 8.0–5-way jct. Turn left up gated Indian Creek Road. It's more of a trail than a road.
- Mile 8.7–take lower right fork through field.
- Mile 8.8–turn left across top of timber cut.
- Mile 11.1–finish.

★ =Start

Farlow Gap

4000'
3000'
2000'

Indian Cr Rd

Summey Cove

*F*ollowing the upper reaches of the French Broad River, this route takes you to a hidden 60-ft. waterfall. Don't let the distance fool you; there is one very steep hill climb.

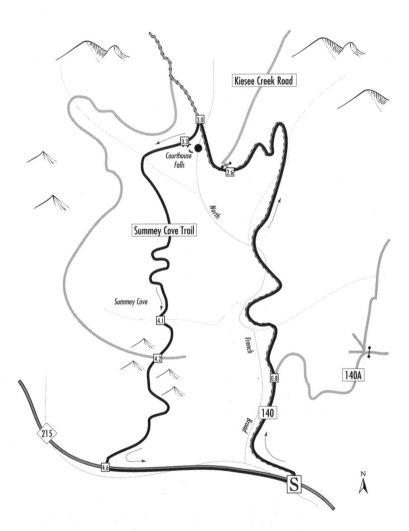

START/FINISH
Jct of NC 215 and FS 140. This is 6.6 miles south of the Blue Ridge Parkway and 1 mile north of Balsam Grove on NC 215.

TRAIL CONFIGURATION
Loop

SURFACE
Single track • 1.6 miles
Forest road • 3 miles
Pavement • 1.4 miles

HIGHLIGHTS
Cascades, Courthouse Falls, very steep uphill and downhill, great views

TOTAL DISTANCE
6 miles

TIME ALLOWANCE
Beginner • 3.5 hours
Intermediate • 2.5 hours
Advanced • 1.5 hours

Mileposts

- From start–ride north up FS 140.
- Mile 0.8–FS 140A enters from right, stay left beside river.
- Mile 2.6–Kiesee Creek Road enters from right. Bear left, downhill.
- Mile 3.0–bottom of hill. Cross bridge and turn left onto Summey Cove Trail (white blazes).
- Mile 3.3–Courthouse Falls Trail turns off to left. (it's a short hike to base of the falls–foot travel only).
- Mile 4.1–cross creek and start steep hill climb.
- Mile 4.2–cross logging road.
- Mile 4.6–jct. NC 215, turn left.
- Mile 6–finish.

Flat Laurel Creek

Starting in the high meadows between Shining Rock and Middle Prong Wilderness, this ride connects with the Blue Ridge Parkway, passes the Devil's Courthouse, and goes through a tunnel. Don't let the first quarter mile of washout intimidate you. Things smooth out, and all the single track is downhill.

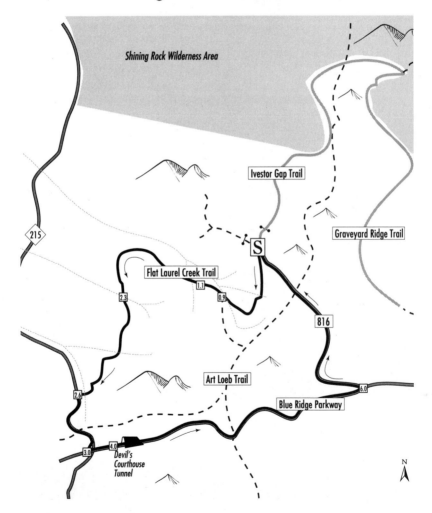

START/FINISH
Trailhead parking area for Black Balsam at end of FS 816 off the Blue Ridge Parkway

TRAIL CONFIGURATION
Loop

SURFACE
Single track • 2.6 miles
Pavement • 4.6 miles

HIGHLIGHTS
Waterfalls, creek crossings, cliff views, high meadows, rocky trail, Blue Ridge Parkway, Devil's Courthouse tunnel

TOTAL DISTANCE
7.2 miles

TIME ALLOWANCE
Beginner • 3 hours
Intermediate • 2.25 hrs
Advanced • 1.5 hours

SPECIAL NOTE
Front lights and rear reflectors are required for riding bicycles through tunnels on the Blue Ridge Parkway

Mileposts

- From start–ride out back of parking lot onto Flat Laurel Creek Trail. The first mile is very rocky.
- Mile 0.9–cross creek and turn right.
- Mile 1.1–look for the waterfall on your right just after passing a flat camping spot.
- Mile 2.3–cross old concrete bridge. You'll see a waterfall on the left, just above the bridge.
- Mile 2.6–cross creek and turn left onto NC 215.
- Mile 3.0–turn left onto Blue Ridge Parkway.
- Mile 4.0–Devil's Courthouse and tunnel.
- Mile 6.0–turn left onto FS 816 to Black Balsam.
- Mile 7.2–finish.

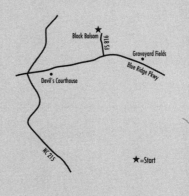

Ivestor Gap

Bordering the Shining Rock Wilderness, this rocky old road bed traverses the high ridges above Wash Hollow and Graveyard Fields. The trail is practically level, but it's so full of boulders that riding it is a real challenge. Blueberries abound in late August. And remember, you can turn around anytime you like.

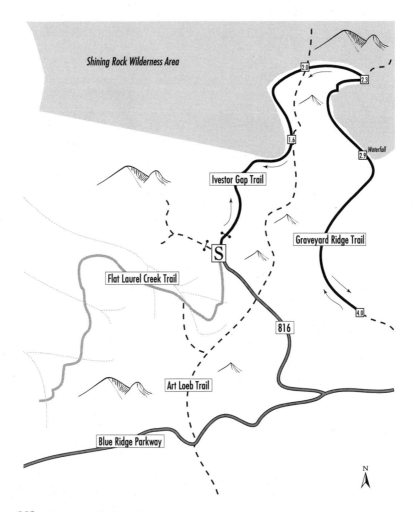

Shining Rock Wilderness Area

2.0

2.3

1.6

Waterfall
2.9

Ivestor Gap Trail

Graveyard Ridge Trail

S

Flat Laurel Creek Trail

4.0

816

Art Loeb Trail

Blue Ridge Parkway

N

START/FINISH
Trailhead parking area for Black Balsam at end of FS 816 off the Blue Ridge Parkway

TRAIL CONFIGURATION
Out-and-Back

SURFACE
Double track • 8 miles

HIGHLIGHTS
No hills, very rocky, slow riding, high meadows, waterfall, berries in season, wet areas

Total Distance
8 miles

TIME ALLOWANCE
Beginner • 3 hours
Intermediate • 2.5 hours
Advanced • 2 hours

Mileposts

- From start–ride through gate out Ivestor Gap Trail (the gate to this old road is open from mid-August through December for berry pickers and hunters).
- Mile 1.6–junction Art Loeb Trail. Stay left on old road.
- Mile 2.0–Ivestor Gap and Wilderness boundary (no bikes are allowed in wilderness areas). Follow old road to right of Wilderness Area.
- Mile 2.3–take a sharp right turn onto Graveyard Ridge Trail.
- Mile 2.9–waterfall to left (if you don't see it, you can hear it).
- Mile 4.0–deep washout. Road bed turns into foot trail. Turn around; bikes are not allowed on the trail from here to Graveyard Fields and the Blue Ridge Parkway.
- Mile 8.0–finish.

Bent Creek Area

Just southwest and barely outside the city limits of Asheville you'll find the Bent Creek Experimental Forest—a 6000-acre tract of land encompassing almost the entire Bent Creek watershed. Part of the Pisgah National Forest, it is more specifically the headquarters and field laboratory for a work unit of the Southern Research Station. Its primary purpose is for the study of silviculture (forest cultivation). This work has been going on for over 70 years, and visitors to the forest are likely to see varous aspects of research in progress. With its close proximity to Asheville, its network of trails, and its camping, hunting, and fishing opportunities, it is also a major recreational site.

Bent Creek sees understandibly heavy use, given its location. Most any day you're likely to see fellow cyclists, runners, joggers, hikers, walkers, fishermen, campers, sightseers, and (in season) hunters

(Farther out and higher up where the terrain is more challenging, use tends to thin out considerably). The closer you are to the trailheads, the more folks you're likely to see. Because of such heavy use, it is very important to remember and follow the "rules of the trail" listed earlier in this book. The trail users around Asheville have done a great job of maintaining harmony, and would like to keep it that way.

Riding in Bent Creek is great fun. Forest Route 479 bisects the area and on both sides there are plenty of trails to choose from. If you're riding on the north side of the road, you may begin to feel that every trail there is named "Sidehill". That's not actually the case, but since most all of them are on the side of the hill (or mountain), it's easy to understand how many sections of trail garnered that name. On the other side of the

(continues)

Bent Creek Area

road and around Lake Powhatan Campground you'll find that many trails are designated for seasonal use only, so keep that in mind as you plan out your routes.

Unlike the rest of Pisgah, Bent Creek has quite a few unnamed trails. Some were even built without authorization by the Forest Service. These have not been included in any of the routes suggested in this book, yet since they do intersect the routes, some are shown on the maps. In addition, Bent Creek is presently undergoing an assessment period. It's possible that some trails that are not now "legal" trails will become "legal" in the future and trails that are now open to bikes could be closed to bikes.

On a smaller tract of land adjacent to the experimental forest is the North Carolina Arboretum. Here you'll find extensive gardens of native shrubs, trees and flowers. There's a huge visitor center and a greenhouse to explore. This is also one of the best places in the area for beginning mountain bikers. Wide trails along the lower stretch of Bent Creek and elsewhere on the property make for excellent, rather easy riding.

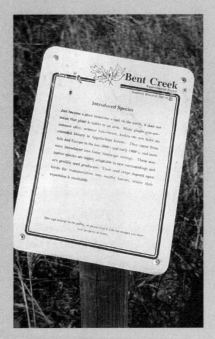

Lower Bent Creek
Owl Ridge
Hardtimes Road
Rice Pinnacle-Ledford
Deerfield-Pine Tree-Explorer
South Ridge Road
Southside
North Boundary
Little Hickory
Ingles Field Gap
Lower Sidehill
Old Sidehill

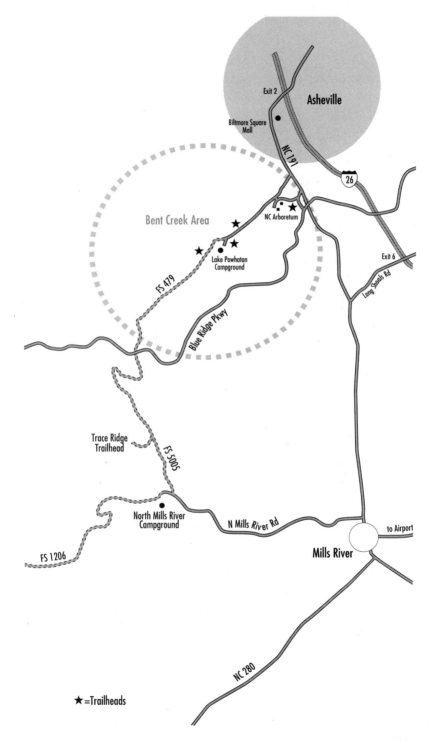

Asheville

Exit 2

Biltmore Square Mall

NC 191

26

NC Arboretum

Bent Creek Area

★

★ ★

Lake Powhatan Campground

FS 479

Blue Ridge Pkwy

Exit 6

Long Shoals Rd

Trace Ridge Trailhead

FS 5005

North Mills River Campground

N Mills River Rd

to Airport

FS 1206

Mills River

NC 280

★ =Trailheads

Lower Bent Creek

*J*ust got that new mountain bike or want to take the kids out for a spin and skip the single track? This is the ride for you. You'll go from the pretty arboretum grounds, out and around Lake Powhatan, and back alongside gentle lower Bent Creek. There are only a few hills to climb, a rarity in these parts.

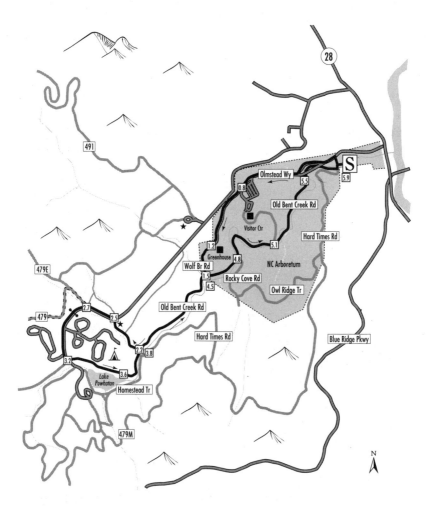

START/FINISH

Recreation Parking Area at the entrance to NC Arboretum. The arboretum is at the jct. of NC 191 and the Blue Ridge Parkway.

TRAIL CONFIGURATION

Double Lollipop Loop

SURFACE

Forest road • 4 miles
Pavement • 1.9 miles

HIGHLIGHTS

Flora and fauna of Arboretum, lake and stream views, few hills

TOTAL DISTANCE

5.9 miles

TIME ALLOWANCE

Beginner • 1+ hours
Intermediate • 1 hour
Advanced • 30 min

Mileposts

- From start–ride into the arboretum on FL Olstead Way.
- 0.8–pass by (or stop in at) the arboretum visitor center.
- Mile 1.2–pass by (or stop in at) the green house and onto the dirt Wolf Branch Road.
- Mile 1.5–turn right and pass through gate onto Old Bent Creek Road.
- Mile 2.2–turn right to Hardtimes Trailhead parking lot.
- Mile 2.5–Hardtimes Trailhead. Turn left on paved road.
- Mile 2.7–turn left into Lake Powhatan Campground.
- Mile 3.2–turn left on the fisherman's access road.
- Mile 3.6–spillway. Continue over dirt hump. Head down creek.
- Mile 3.8–pass turn to Hardtimes.
- Mile 4.5–pass through gate and bear right to remain by creek.
- Mile 4.8–Rocky Cove Road enters from right. Continue straight on.
- Mile 5.1–Running Cedar Road enters from left. Stay straight.
- Mile 5.5–just before pavement, turn right across wooden bridge and then turn immediately left and head under roadway.
- Mile 5.9–finish.

Visitor Ctr

Lake Powhatan

2000'

1000'

Owl Ridge

Here's a short route that is a good introduction to both climbing hills and trail riding. It is entirely within the NC Arboretum, so it makes a great hunting season option as well. You'll climb partway to the Parkway on a dirt road and then drop down an undulating double track to finish alongside Bent Creek.

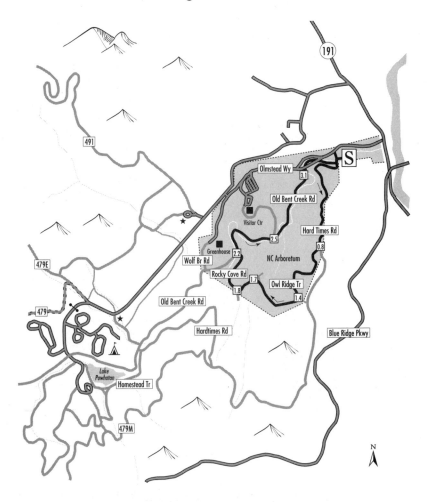

START/FINISH
Recreation Parking Area at the entrance to the NC Arboretum. The Arboretum is at the jct. of NC 191 and the Blue Ridge Parkway

TRAIL CONFIGURATION
Loop

SURFACE
Double track • 1 mile
Forest road • 2.5 miles

HIGHLIGHTS
Close to a mile of steady climb, some loose gravel, spotty views, stream view, arboretum flora & fauna

TOTAL DISTANCE
3.5 miles

TIME ALLOWANCE
Beginner • 1+ hours
Intermediate • 45 min
Advanced • 30 min

Mileposts

• From start–ride around gate and up Hardtimes Road.
• Mile 0.8–turn right on Owl Ridge Trail (blue plastic blazes).
• Mile 1.4–bear right as you enter an old road. You'll see a gate up to the left.
• Mile 1.7–pass a jumble of old roads on your right. Bear left at each and head downhill.
• Mile 1.8–turn right on Rocky Cove Road. An authorized personel only road heads to the left.
• Mile 2.2–turn right on Old Bent Creek Road.
• Mile 2.5–Running Cedar Road enters from the left.
• Mile 3.1–just before pavement, turn right across wooden bridge and then turn immediately left and head under roadway.
• Mile 3.5–finish.

★=Start
Bent Creek Ranch Rd
NC 191
Visiter Ctr
NC Arboretum
Blue Ridge Pkwy

Jct Owl Ridge Tr

Bent Creek Rd

2000'
1000'

Hardtimes Road

***F**or most cyclists, the name of this ride does not denote its nature. This popular route is none too hard as it climbs the same spine as the Blue Ridge Parkway. You'll pass a spring (look for the pipe sticking out of the bank) and get a great view of the Asheville skyline. It finishes up alongside meandering Bent Creek.*

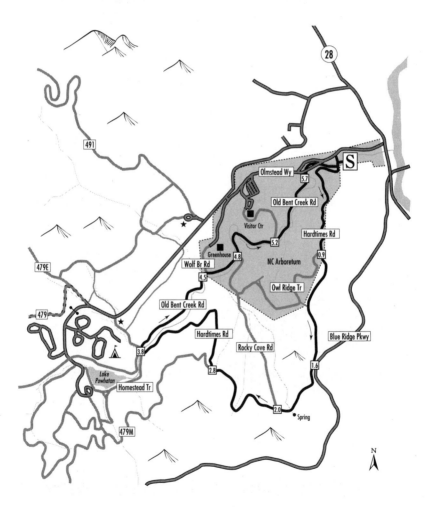

START/FINISH
Recreation Parking Area
at the entrance to
NC Arboretum. The
arboretum is at the
jct. of NC 191
and the Blue Ridge
Parkway

TRAIL CONFIGURATION
Loop

SURFACE
Forest Road • 6 miles

HIGHLIGHTS
All forest roads, spotty
views, spring, parallels
Blue Ridge Parkway,
some loose gravel

TOTAL DISTANCE
6 miles

TIME ALLOWANCE
Beginner • 2+ hours
Intermediate • 1.25 hrs
Advanced • 45 min

Mileposts

- From start–ride around gate and up Hardtimes Road.
- Mile 0.8–Owl Ridge Trail exits on the right. Stay on road.
- Mile 0.9–pass through gate.
- Mile 1.6–parallel the Blue Ridge Parkway. Mountains to Sea/Shut-in Ridge Trail shares road for a short ways.
- Mile 2.0–you'll find the spring and an old cistern on the left here. Just up ahead an old section of Rocky Cove Road enters from the right. Don't take it.
- Mile 2.8–bear right to remain on Hardtimes Road
- Mile 3.8–cross bridge and turn right on Old Bent Creek Road.
- Mile 4.5–pass through gate and bear right to remain by creek.
- Mile 4.8–Rocky Cove Road enters from the right. Stay straight.
- Mile 5.2–Running Cedar Road enters from the left. Stay straight.
- Mile 5.7–just before pavement, turn right across wooden bridge and then turn immediately left and head under roadway.
- Mile 6.0–finish.

Rice Pinnacle-Ledford

The majority of this ride is on forest roads, including all the climbs and descents, which moderates its difficulty. Some may find the last stretch of single track a bit technical. It parallels the paved road, so if you prefer, you can finish up that way instead.

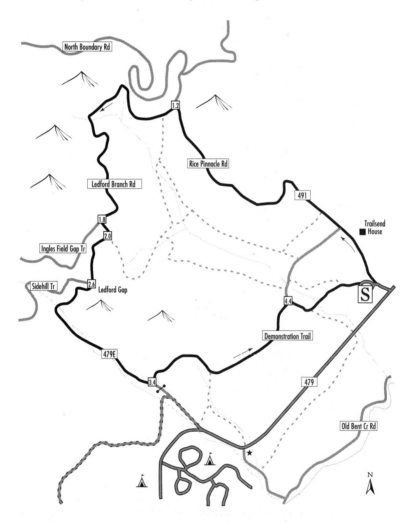

START/FINISH

Rice Pinnacle Trailhead Parking. This is the first trailhead you come to, once you enter Bent Creek Experimental Forest.

TRAIL CONFIGURATION

Loop

SURFACE

Single track • 1.4 miles
Forest road • 3.4 miles

HIGHLIGHTS

Forest road climbs and descents, some loose gravel, spotty views, rooty sections

TOTAL DISTANCE

4.8 miles

TIME ALLOWANCE

Beginner • 1.5 hours
Intermediate • 1 hour
Advanced • 45 min

Mileposts

- From start–ride out of parking area and up Rice Pinnacle Road (FS 491).
- Mle 1.2–turn left on Ledford Branch Road (FS 479E).
- Mile 1.8–Ingles Field Gap exits on the right.
- Mile 2.0–an unmarked road exits downhill on the left.
- Mile 2.6–Ledford Gap. There's a resting bench here (if you're tired) and Sidehill Trail exits to the right.
- Mile 3.4–turn left on the single track trail. It's just before you get to the gate for FS 479E. A number of smaller trails exit off the right side of this trail. Bear left at each one, including the powerline cut.
- Mile 4.4–turn right on the old roadbed that takes you alongside an overgrown and drained pond area.
- Mile 4.8–finish (the last short stretch of trail is paved!).

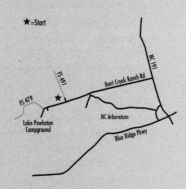

★ =Start

Ledford Br Rd   Ledford Gap

2000'
1000'

Deerfield-Pine Tree-Explorer

This is a fun loop using Bent Creek's more popular seasonal trails. Parts follow the Demonstration Trail where you'll find interpretive signs describing aspects of the forest. Expect to see other trail users on this ride.

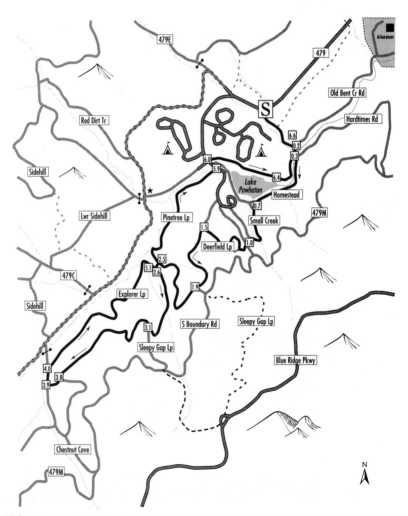

START/FINISH

Hardtimes Trailhead Parking. This is the second trailhead you come to once you enter Bent Creek

TRAIL CONFIGURATION

Figure 8

SURFACE

Single/double track • 6.8 miles

HIGHLIGHTS

Technical roots sections, old homesite, lake view, interpretive signs, all single track, wooden bridges

TOTAL DISTANCE

6.8 miles

TIME ALLOWANCE

Beginner • 3 hours
Intermediate • 2.5 hours
Advanced • 1.5 hours

SEASONAL TRAIL OPEN OCT 15 – APR 15

Mileposts

- From start–ride around gate and down Hardtimes Road
- Mile 0.2–turn right on Old Bent Creek Road.
- Mile 0.3–turn left across bridge and then right on Homestead Trail (orange blaze).
- Mile 0.7–trail forks. Bear left up Small Creek Trail (red blaze).
- Mile 1.0–two trails enter from the right. Go up wood steps and straight onto Deerfield Loop Trail (yellow blaze).
- Mile 1.5–turn left onto Pine Tree Loop Trail (blue blaze).
- Mile 1.9–Sleepy Gap Loop Trail. enters from the left. Stay straight.
- Mile 2.5–turn left on connector.
- Mile 2.6–turn left on Explorer Loop Trail (yellow blaze).
- Mile 3.1–other end of Sleepy Gap Loop Trail enters from left.
- Mile 3.8–go straight onto Explorer Alternate Trail.
- Mile 3.9–turn right on dirt road.
- Mile 4.0–turn right on Explorer Loop Trail.
- Mile 5.1–turn left on Connector and then left on Pine Tree Loop Tr.
- Mile 5.9–turn left across Bent Creek on campground road.
- Mile 6–turn right on fisherman's access road beside lake.
- Mile 6.4–at spillway, go over dirt hump and continue by creek.
- Mile 6.6–turn left to trailhead.
- Mile 6.8–finish.

| Deerfield Loop Tr | Pine Tree Loop Tr | Explorer Loop Tr | Pine Tree Loop Tr |

2000'

1000'

South Ridge Road

A long steady forest road climb sets the mood for the first seven miles of this ride. You'll like the views and sweeping turns. Once you cross to the other side of the watershed, it's a single track return on Lower Sidehill where the riding is a little more technical.

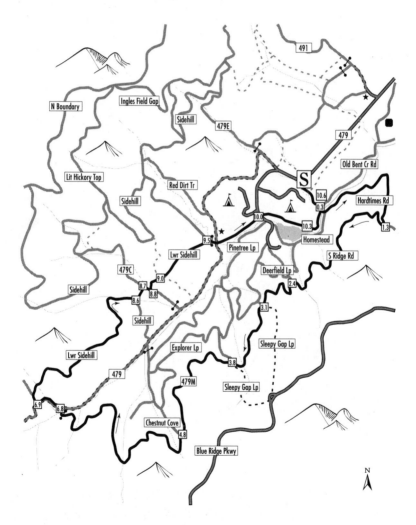

START/FINISH
Hardtimes Trailhead Parking. This is the second trailhead you come to once you enter Bent Creek.

TRAIL CONFIGURATION
Loop

SURFACE
Single track • 3.3 miles
Forest road • 7.6 miles

HIGHLIGHTS
Long steady climb, spotty views, short technical section on trail, downhill single track

TOTAL DISTANCE
10.9 miles

TIME ALLOWANCE
Beginner • 3.5 hours
Intermediate • 2.5 hours
Advanced • 1.5 hours

Mileposts

- From start–ride around gate and down Hardtimes Road.
- Mile 0.3–turn right and then left across the bridge to remain on Hardtimes Road.
- Mile 2.4–Deerfield Trail exits right.
- Mile 3.1–Sleepy Gap Loop crosses.
- Mile 3.8–Sleepy Gap Loop crosses.
- Mile 4.8–Chestnut Cove Trail exits on the right.
- Mile 6.8–turn left on FS 479.
- Mile 6.9–turn right on Lower Sidehill Trail (orange blaze).
- Mile 8.6– bear left as Sidehill Trail enters from the right.
- Mile 8.7–turn right on FS 479C.
- Mile 8.8–turn left up past old gate to continue on Lower Sidehill.
- Mile 9.0–at a Y-intersection, an unmarked trail exits to the left and then at the next Y one exits to the right.
- Mile 9.5–turn right on forest road, pass gate, cross FS 479 and continue onto Campground Connector Trail.
- Mile 10.0–cross on to fisherman's access road.
- Mile 10.3–spillway. Go over dirt hump and along creek.
- Mile 10.6–turn left to trailhead.
- Mile 10.9–finish.

S Ridge Rd

Jct Lwr Sidehill

2000'

1000'

Southside

A number of nice trails drop off of South Ridge Road. Here's the best way to try them all in one ride. In keeping with the "Sidehill" tradition of Bent Creek, I called this ride Southside and omitted the "hill"—in name only, though, because it's still very hilly!

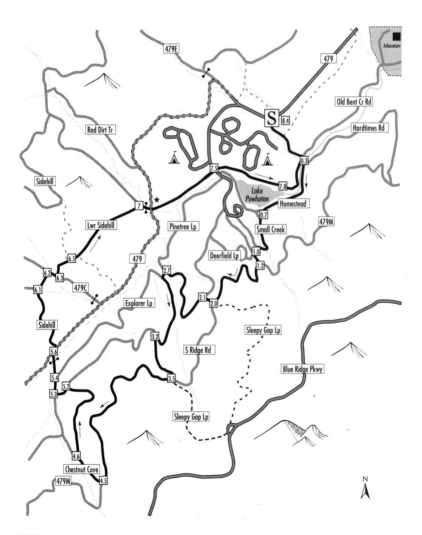

START/FINISH
Hardtimes Trailhead Parking. This is the second trailhead you see once you enter Bent Creek.

TRAIL CONFIGURATION
Loop

SURFACE
Single track • 6 miles
Forest road • 2.4 miles

HIGHLIGHTS
Great single track, short and steep ups and downs, rooty section, interpretive signs

TOTAL DISTANCE
8.4 miles

SEASONAL TRAIL
OPEN OCT 15 – APR 15

Mileposts

- From start–ride around gate and down Hardtimes Road.
- Mile 0.3–turn right, then left. across the bridge, then right onto Homestead Trail (orange blaze).
- Mile 0.7–bear left up Small Cr Tr.
- Mile 1.0–trails jct. Turn left and ride up Deerfield Trail (it gets steep).
- Mile 1.2–turn right on S Ridge Rd.
- Mile 2.0–turn right down Sleepy Gap Loop Trail (red blaze).
- Mile 2.1–turn left on Pine Tree Lp.
- Mile 2.7–turn left on the connector and then left on Explorer Lp.
- Mile 3.2–turn left up Sleepy Gap.
- Mile 3.5–turn right on S Ridge Rd.
- Mile 4.5–turn right down Chestnut Cove Trail.
- Mile 4.6–bear right onto Explorer.
- Mile 5.2–turn left on Explorer Alt.
- Mile 5.3–turn right on forest road.
- Mile 5.4–pass Explorer Loop.
- Mile 5.6–cross FS 479 onto Sidehill Trail (orange blaze).
- Mile 6.1–bear right onto Lower Sidehill (orange blaze).
- Mile 6.2–turn right on FS 479C.
- Mile 6.3–turn left past old gate back onto Lower Sidehill.
- Mile 6.5–at Y bear right and at the next Y bear left.
- Mile 7–turn right on forest road, cross FS 479 and continue onto Campground Connector.
- Mile 7.5–cross onto fisherman's access road.
- Mile 7.8–spillway. Ride over dirt hump and continue by creek.
- Mile 8.1–turn left to trailhead.
- Mile 8.4–finish.

S Ridge Rd   S Ridge Rd   Lwr Sidehill

2000'
1000'

North Boundary

*Y*ou'll enjoy this one going either direction, so when you finish it one way, turn around and ride it in reverse. Either way, you'll ride up (and I mean up!) to the northern boundary of the forest, only to make a spinning descent back to the start.

N Boundary Rd

3.9

3.8

491

3.1

Ingles Field Gap   Ingles Field Gap Tr
6.4   7.1
2.4
Ledford Gap

485   Connector Tr

7.4   479E

Sidehill Tr

7.9   1.6

1.4

Red Dirt Tr   1.3
★
1.0

Boyd Br Rd   8.6

0.4   0.7

Sidehill   Connector   L Powhatan

S

Lower Sidehill   Deerfield Tr

479C   479   Pinetree Tr

Old Sidehill   N

Sidehill   Explorer Tr

Lower Sidehill   479M

Mileposts

START/FINISH
Jct. of Campground
Connector Trail,
FS 479, and gated
Boyd Branch Road

TRAIL CONFIGURATION
Loop

SURFACE
Single track • 5.1 miles
Forest road • 3.8 miles

HIGHLIGHTS
Long climb, long
downhill, whoops,
good views

TOTAL DISTANCE
8.9 miles

TIME ALLOWANCE
Beginner • 3 hours
Intermediate • 2 hours
Advanced • 1.25 hours

- From start–ride down Campground Connector.
- Mile 0.4–cross onto fisherman's access road.
- Mile 0.7–spillway. Go over hump.
- Mile 1.0–turn left on Hardtimes Rd.
- Mile 1.3–turn left on pavement.
- Mile 1.4–go right at road fork. Don't go into campground.
- Mile 1.6–bear right onto FS 479E.
- Mile 2.4–Ledford Gap. Bear right. Sidehill Trail exits left.
- Mile 3.1–pass a road on the right then Ingles Field Gap Trail on left.
- Mile 3.8–turn left on FS 491.
- Mile 3.9–continue straight onto North Boundary Road.
- Mile 6.4–Ingles Field Gap. Turn hard left onto Ingles Field Gap Trail (blue blaze).
- Mile 7.1–turn right on Connector Trail (orange blaze).
- Mile 7.4–turn right on Sidehill Trail (yellow blaze).
- Mile 7.9–turn left on Red Dirt Trail.
- Mile 8.6–turn right on FS 479.
- Mile 8.9–finish.

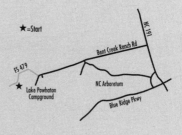

★ =Start

NC 191

Bent Creek Ranch Rd

FS 479

NC Arboretum

Lake Powhatan
Campground

Blue Ridge Pkwy

N Boundary Rd   Ingles Field Gap

Hardtimes Trailhead

2000'

1000'

Little Hickory

*T*his nice ride that climbs to Ingles Field Gap is somewhat tough, but also a lot of fun since there is so much
downhill that follows. Much of the track is smooth with
the occasional sprinkling of rocks and roots. The last
part is on a seasonal trail, but you can always finish up
on Lower Sidehill or down FS 479.

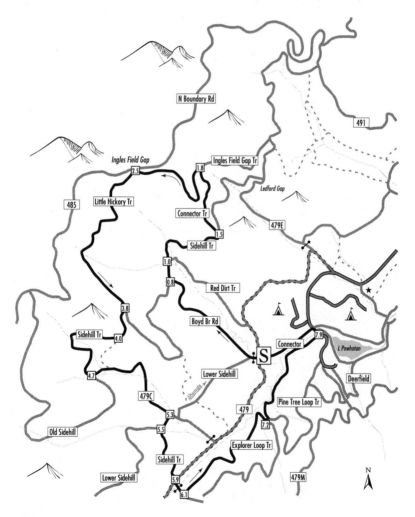

START/FINISH
Jct. of Campground
Connector Trail,
FS 479, and gated
Boyd Branch Road

TRAIL CONFIGURATION
Loop

SURFACE
Single track • 7.3 miles
Forest road • 1 mile

HIGHLIGHTS
Small stream crossings,
occasional whoops,
rhodo and hemlock
tunnels, roots and rocks

TOTAL DISTANCE
8.3 miles

TIME ALLOWANCE
Beginner • 2.5–3 hours
Intermediate • 2 hours
Advanced • 1.25 hours

USES SEASONAL TRAIL
OPEN OCT 15 – APR 15

Mileposts

- From start–ride up and around gate onto Boyd Branch Road.
- Mile 0.8–Sidehill Trail exits left.
- Mile 1.0–end of road. Continue onto Sidehill Trail (yellow blaze).
- Mile 1.5–turn left up Connector to Ingles Field Gap (orange blaze).
- Mile 1.8–turn left on Ingles Field Gap Trail (blue blaze).
- Mile 2.5–Ingles Field Gap. Bear to the left down Little Hickory Trail (yellow blaze).
- Mile 3.8–bear right onto Sidehill Trail (yellow blaze).
- Mile 4.0–unnamed trail goes left.
- Mile 4.7–bear left to stay on Sidehill and then continue onto FS 479C down the hill.
- Mile 5.3–turn right on Lower Sidehill (orange blaze).
- Mile 5.5–just past stream crossing, turn left on Sidehill (not marked).
- Mile 5.9–bear right and then left to cross FS 479 onto gated road.
- Mile 6.1–turn left on Explorer Loop Trail (yellow blaze).
- Mile 7.2–bear left on Connector and then left on Pine Tree Loop.
- Mile 7.9–turn left and then left again toward dump station and onto Campground Connector.
- Mile 8.3–finish.

Ingles Field Gap

Explorer/Pine Tree

2000'

1000'

Ingles Field Gap

This is a moderate ride with some really fun single track. The climbs and descents are very gradual while at times the trail is rocky. You'll especially enjoy the views and the small whoops on the way down.

Mileposts

- From start–ride up past gate onto Boyd Branch Road.
- Mile 0.8–turn left on Sidehill Trail (yellow blaze).
- Mile 1.5–trail splits. Bear right, up the hill.
- Mile 2.0–bear right at inverted Y onto Little Hickory Trail (yellow).
- Mile 2.7–an unmarked trail exits down the hill on the right.
- Mile 3.3–Ingles Field Gap. Turn right and then immediately right on Ingles Field Gap Trail (blue).
- Mile 4–Connector Trail exits right; stay straight.
- Mile 5.2–turn right on FS 479E.
- Mile 5.3–bear right as double track exits left.
- Mile 5.9–Ledford Gap. There is a picnic table here. Turn right on Sidehill Trail (yellow blaze).
- Mile 6.7–Connector Trail enters from right; stay straight.
- Mile 7.2–turn left onto unmarked Red Dirt Trail.
- Mile 7.8–turn right on FS 479.
- Mile 8.1–finish.

START/FINISH
Jct. of Campground Connector Trail, FS 479, and gated Boyd Branch Road

TRAIL CONFIGURATION
Loop

SURFACE
Single track • 7.1 miles
Forest road • 1 miles

HIGHLIGHTS
Spotty views, small stream crossings, interpretive signs, small whoops, rocky sections

TOTAL DISTANCE
8.1 miles

TIME ALLOWANCE
Beginner • 3 hours
Intermediate • 2.5 hours
Advanced • 1.5 hours

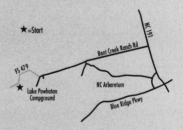

Ingles Field Gap

2000'
1000'

Lower Sidehill

*Y*ou may want to use this as a prelude to taking on more of Bent Creek's trails. The warm-up begins with a forest road climb followed by a short, steep, rocky ascent onto Lower Sidehill. The last half is all downhill. In the winter, you may want to use seasonal Pine Tree Loop and Explorer Loop Trails instead of FS 479.

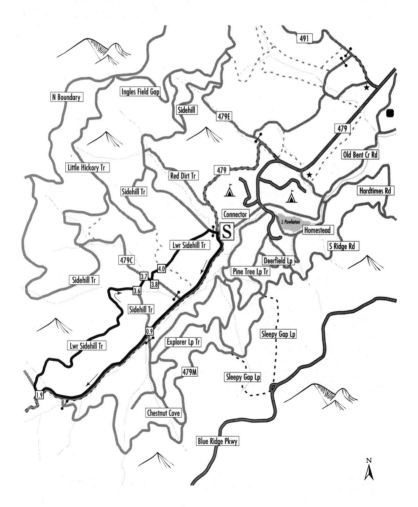

Mileposts

START/FINISH
Jct. of Campground
Connector Trail,
FS 479, and gated
Boyd Branch Road

TRAIL CONFIGURATION
Loop

SURFACE
Single track • 2.6 miles
Forest road • 1.9 miles

HIGHLIGHTS
Loose gravel on forest
road, small stream
crossings, wildlife fields,
experimental areas,
spotty views, boggy
section

TOTAL DISTANCE
4.5 miles

TIME ALLOWANCE
Beginner • 1.25+ hours
Intermediate • <1 hour
Advanced • 30 min

- From start–ride southwest on FS 479 (away from the campground).
- Mile 0.9–Sidehill Trail exits road on the right.
- Mile 1.9–turn right on Lower Sidehill (orange blaze). The first section is steep and rocky.
- Mile 3.6–Sidehill Trail enters from right. Bear left and cross stream.
- Mile 3.7–turn right on FS 479C.
- Mile 3.8–turn left up past old gate to continue on Lower Sidehill Trail.
- Mile 4.0–you will come to two Y intersections. Bear right at the first one and left at the second one.
- Mile 4.5–turn right and go down past the gate to finish.

Jct Lower Sidehill

2000'

1000'

If you're looking for a really difficult ride in Bent Creek, this might just fit the bill. It has a lot of climbing, a steep, loose, rock downhill, and some technical washouts to negotiate. The section along North Boundary Road tends to get overgrown in summer.

From Ingles Field Gap going up TMF, 1ST ⓛ is Betty Heinous and 2nd ⓛ is MO' Heinous.

START/FINISH
Jct. of Campground
Connector Trail,
FS 479, and gated
Boyd Branch Road

TRAIL CONFIGURATION
Loop

SURFACE
Single track • 8 miles
Forest road • 0.4 miles

HIGHLIGHTS
Long climb, loose rocks,
washouts, steep down-
hill, spotty views,
hidden trail entrance

TOTAL DISTANCE
8.4 miles

TIME ALLOWANCE
Beginner • not advised
Intermediate • 2.5 hours
Advanced • 1.5 hours

Mileposts

- From start–ride northeast on FS 479 (up the hill).
- Mile 0.2–turn left on Red Dirt Trail. It's marked with a trail sign, but there is no name on the sign.
- Mile 0.9–turn left on Boyd Br Rd.
- Mile 1.0–turn right on Sidehill Trail (yellow blaze).
- Mile 1.8–bear right as unmarked trail exits left.
- Mile 2.3–go right on Little Hickory Tr.
- Mile 2.9–unmarked trail on right.
- Mile 3.6–Ingles Field Gap. Go left on North Bounday Road.
- Mile 5.0–turn right on unmarked trail. It is very steep.
- Mile 6.2–bear hard left as an old roadbed enters from right.
- Mile 6.9–Sidehill Trail enters from the left, continue on and onto FS 479C down the hill.
- Mile 7.5–pass Lower Sidehill on the right.
- Mile 7.6–turn left up past old gate onto Lower Sidehill (orange).
- Mile 7.8–you will come to two Y intersections. Bear right at the first one and left at the second one.
- Mile 8.4–turn right and go down past the gate to finish.

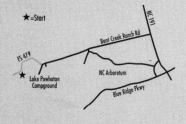

★ = Start

NC 191

Bent Creek Ranch Rd

FS 479

Lake Powhatan Campground

NC Arboretum

Blue Ridge Pkwy

3000'
2000'
1000'

Ingles Field Gap

Old Sidehill Tr

Dupont State Forest

*L*ocated just south of Brevard and the Pisgah National Forest, Dupont is one of North Carolina's newest state forests. It is also the most popular, and has quickly become a mecca for mountain bikers. Boasting a number of large waterfalls, several pristine lakes, and close to 100 miles of trails, you'll find the area considerably different in look and feel than the other areas covered in this book.

Some of the things you'll see in Dupont will cause you to wonder, so here is a very brief history that may help explain a few of them. Dupont was not always a state forest. The Dupont Corporation owned the land for many years. During its tenure, the Dupont Corporation created a number of lakes and put in an airstrip so Dupont executives, friends and associates could have a secluded tract of land to enjoy in the mountains. People who lived nearby also used the land for various forms of recreation. The spectacular falls were a wonder to see. Hikers enjoyed the trails to the top of Cedar Rock Mountain. Hunters and fishermen found game abundant and fished the streams and lakes. In 1996 the state of North Carolina purchased a large portion of the land to form the new state forest. Another portion, that surrounding the current AGFA plant, was bought by Diagnostic Imaging. This area included five of the tract's beautiful (and very large) waterfalls. The

(continues)

Dupont State Forest

state attempted to buy these lands as well, but eventually the tract was acquired by a private developer and plans were made for construction of luxury homesites. The public would no longer be welcome.

A grassroots group named Friends of the Falls organized to halt the development of this pristine property with unique geographical features. One thing led to another and in the end the state of North Carolina, led by the governor, invoked its power of eminent domain and purchased the property. The development was halted, but not before a number of roads were hurriedly built and several buildings were partially constructed. There is even a covered bridge crossing the Little River directly above High Falls!

BIKERS WILL FIND PLENTY OF TRAILS TO CHOOSE FROM

Mountain bikers visiting Dupont will find a large network of trails and roads—so many that it can be confusing. There are no fewer than 98 of them. Some are quite short, while others traverse vast portions of the forest. Interestingly, many of the roads are named as trails and the trails are

named as roads. for instance, you'll find that Lake Imaging Trail is most definitely a road, while much of Corn Mill Shoals Road is single track trail! It hardly matters; road or trail, they're all great fun to ride.

From the outset, Dupont has welcomed cyclists. Even the caretaker is an avid mountain biker. But be aware also that Dupont sees heavy use—especially on pretty weekends. Users have a number trailheads to choose from, and you'll find the different groups tend to separate themselves out. Horseback riders most frequently use the Flatwoods trailhead and ride in that general area. It's not uncommon to see the Flatwoods parking area full of horse trailers on nice weekend days. Day hikers tend to concentrate around the waterfalls and start out from the Staton Road trailhead and the Buck Forest trailhead. Bike riding on the section of Triple Falls Trail nearest the river and on High Falls trail is not recommended in this book due to the concentration of walkers and hikers there. Mountain bikers tend to start out from the Cascade Lake Road trailhead as well as the Buck Forest trailhead. Once in the woods everyone tends to spread out; on many weekdays and even some weekends, you may find few or no other cars in the lot.

VOLUNTEERS IN ACTION

When it comes to trail building, maintenance and conservation, Dupont is a model forest. Most any season you might stumble upon a trail crew at work—and their work really shows. You'll find the trails are well marked with large brown signs at every trail junction. The trails themselves are well drained,

and in any areas where soil erosion is a possibility the trail has either been rerouted or there are plans for doing so. In fact, so much work is ongoing, some trail lengths here will change over time. Be aware that this could alter the directional mileposts for route descriptions in this book.

Should you be interested in volunteering for a morning, an afternoon or a day of trail work, contact the trail work coordinator at either the Friends of Dupont State Forest or the Blue Ridge Bicycle Club listed below:

Dupont State Forest

Friends of Dupont State Forest
PO Box 42
Hendersonville, NC 28793
trailboss@dupontforest.com
www.dupontforest.com

Blue Ridge Bicycle Club
PO Box 309
Asheville, NC 28802
www.blueridgebicycleclub.org

When riding in Dupont, as anywhere, use good judgement. The waterfalls all but invite you to come for a closer look. But be-ware—the closer you get the more slippery the rocks become. For safety's sake, stay off those rocks closest to the falls. Also, keep away from the fragile moss covering portions of the bare rocks. Once trampled upon, it will not grow back.

Special note: As this book went to press, a short section of Conserva-tion Road that crosses AGFA property was in a right-of-way dispute. More than likely it will be worked out by summer of 2002. Routes that use that portion of roadway are not included here, however it is shown on the maps should it be opened in the future.

Cedar Rock
Dupont Epic
Bridal Veil Falls
Waterfalls
Flatwoods Easy
Flatwoods Moderate
Flatwoods Difficult
Grassy-Briery
Casual Dupont

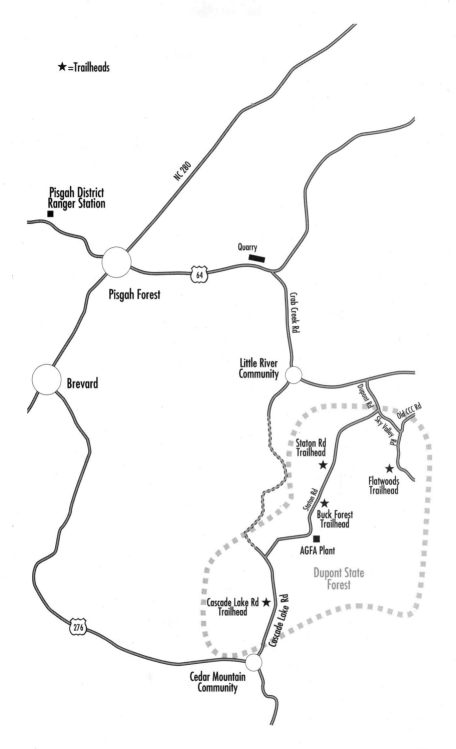

★ =Trailheads

Pisgah District
Ranger Station

NC 280

Quarry

64

Pisgah Forest

Crab Creek Rd

Brevard

Little River
Community

Dupont Rd

Old CCC Rd

Sky Valley Rd

Staton Rd
Trailhead ★

★ Flatwoods
Trailhead

Staton Rd

Buck Forest
Trailhead ★

AGFA Plant ■

Dupont State
Forest

Cascade Lake Rd
Trailhead ★

Cascade Lake Rd

276

Cedar Mountain
Community

Cedar Rock

This ride really has a lot of everything, from smooth single track to large expanses of exposed granite. You might subtitle this ride "Slickrock East." Ascents and descents on expansive slabs of granite can leave you wondering where all the dirt is. Not to worry—this ride also has a classic southeastern descent chock full of loose rock, roots, and sandy washouts.

START/FINISH
Cascade Lake Road
Trailhead Parking

TOTAL DISTANCE
11.3 miles

TIME ALLOWANCE
Beginner • 3.5 hours
Intermediate • 2.5 hours
Advanced • 2 hours

Mileposts

- From Start–take trail to left of parking lot under the powerline.
- Mile 0.1–turn right on Wilkie Tr.
- Mile 0.4–turn right on Micajah Tr.
- Mile 0.8–left on Rock Quarry Rd.
- Mile 1.3–at 5-way intersection, turn left on Buck Ridge Road.
- Mile 2.0–turn left down Micajah Tr.
- Mile 2.4–turn right down Wilkie Tr.
- Mile 2.9–cross road onto Corn Mill Shoals Rd.
- Mile 3.0–Big Rock Trail enters from the left. Stay on CM Shoals Rd.
- Mile 3.6– Burnt Mountain Trail on right. Then Bridal Veil Trail exits to the left. Stay on CM Shoals Road.
- Mile 3.9–Little River Trail exits to the right. Bear left on CM Shoals Rd for short detour to Little River.
- Mile 4.0–view CM Shoals, then go back the way you came in.
- Mile 4.1–left on Little River Trail.
- Mile 5.2–right on Burnt Mtn Tr.
- Mile 6.3–right on C M Shoals Rd. and then bear left on Bridal Veil Trail.
- Mile 6.8–Cedar Rock Trail enters from left. Remain on Bridal Veil Tr.
- Mile 7.5–turn left on other end of Cedar Rock Trail just before the powerline cut.
- Mile 7.7–enter powerline cut. Go about 50 feet into it and then take a sharp left back up the hill and out of the powerline cut on the same side you entered it.
- Mile 8.5–top of Cedar Rock. Follow the rock cairns to the right which leads you onto Big Rock Trail.
- Mile 9.3–turn right on C M Shoals Rd.
- Mile 9.4–bail out or continue by turning right on Longside Trail.
- Mile 9.6–Twixt Trail exits to left.
- Mile 10.2–turn left on Pine Tree Tr.
- Mile 10.4–turn left on roadway.
- Mile 10.6–turn left on Twixt Trail.
- Mile 11.0–bear right on Longside Tr.
- Mile 11.2–right on C M Shoals Tr.
- Mile 11.3–finish.

Dupont Epic

With the multitude of trails in Dupont, the area just begs for epic rides. Here's one that takes in a good deal of the forest, including many of the classic attractions as well as some of the more remote areas. Try this out or make up your own epic. The choices are endless.

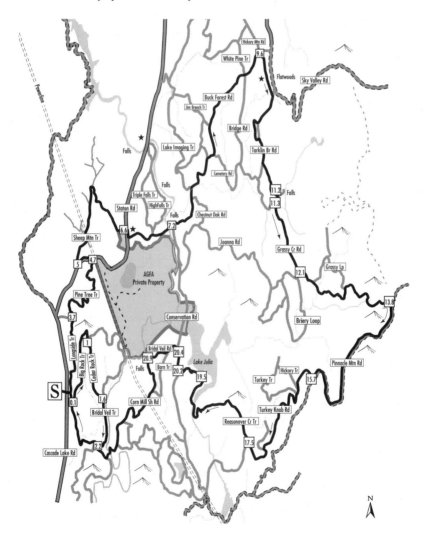

START/FINISH
Cascade Lake Road
Trailhead Parking

TOTAL DISTANCE
23.5 miles

TIME ALLOWANCE
Beginner • not advised
Intermediate • 6 hours
Advanced • 4 hours

Mileposts

- From start–ride across road and onto Corn Mill Shoals Road.
- Mile 0.1–turn left up Big Rock Tr.
- Mile 1.0–top of Cedar Rock Mtn. Follow cairns straight across the rock onto Cedar Rock Trail.
- Mile 1.6–turn right on Bridal Veil Tr.
- Mile 2.2–bear right on Corn Mill Shoals Road.
- Mile 2.9–just past Big Rock Trail, turn right on Longside Trail.
- Mile 3.7–turn right on Pine Tree Tr.
- Mile 4.7–turn left on Staton Rd.
- Mile 5–turn right on Sheep Mtn Tr and follow it around Sheep Mtn.
- Mile 6.6–cross Staton Rd onto Buck Forest Rd (alternate trailhead).
- Mile 7.2–cross Little River at covered bridge. You might want

to make a detour to view the falls. Otherwise follow Buck Forest all the way to the Flatwoods.
- Mile 9.6–turn right toward Flatwoods Trailhead (alt start). Continue onto Tarklin Branch Rd.
- Mile 11.2–you can detour here to see Wintergreen Falls.
- Mile 11.3–turn left across creek onto Grassy Creek Road.
- Mile 12.1–turn left on Joanna Road and continue on it.
- Mile 13.8–turn right on Pinnacle Mountain Road.
- Mile 15.7–right past gate on Turkey Knob Rd. It may not be marked.
- Mile 17.5–bear right on Reasonover Creek Trail.
- Mile 19.5–Lake Julia. Turn left on Lake Julia Road.
- Mile 20.2–right on Conservation Rd.
- Mile 20.4–left on Bridal Veil Rd.
- Mile 20.9–Bridal Veil Falls. Turn left on to Corn Mill Shoals Rd (it's a trail here) and follow to finish.
- Mile 23.5–finish.

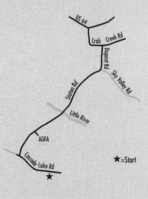

Waterfalls

On this ride you'll see four of the major waterfalls within Dupont, and get a good idea of the development that went awry. Single track trails lead you onto gravel development roads and back onto single track trails. The waterfalls are nothing less than spectacular, and there is ample opportunity to take a break and enjoy their magic.

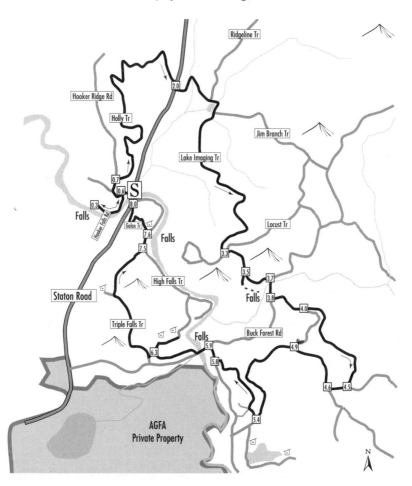

START/FINISH
Staton Road Trailhead
Parking

TRAIL CONFIGURATION
Loop

SURFACE
Single/double track •
6.1 miles
Forest road • 1.7 miles

HIGHLIGHTS
waterfalls, loose gravel,
views, hiker use, horse
use, abandoned
development, short
gutbusting climbs,
covered bridge

TOTAL DISTANCE
7.8 miles

TIME ALLOWANCE
Beginner • 3.5 hours
Intermediate • 2.5 hours
Advanced • 2 hours

Mileposts

- From Start–ride out back of parking lot on Hooker Falls Road.
- Mile 0.3–view Hooker Falls. Turn around here.
- Mile 0.6–left on Hooker Ridge Rd.
- Mile 0.7–bear right to remain on Hooker Ridge Road. Then bear right on Holly Trail.
- Mile 2–right on Staton Road and then left on Lake Imaging Trail.
- Mile 3.3–bear left at the top of a gutbuster of a climb.
- Mile 3.5–turn right to view Grassy Creek Falls.
- Mile 3.7–turn right on Buck Forest.
- Mile 3.8–left on Chestnut Oak Rd.
- Mile 4.0–left on Oak Tree Trail.
- Mile 4.5–turn right on Joanna Rd.
- Mile 4.6–turn right to remain on Joanna Road.
- Mile 4.9–Chestnut Oak Rd enters from the right. Stay on Joanna Rd.
- Mile 5.4–turn right on Pitch Pine Tr.
- Mile 5.8–right on Conservation Rd.
- Mile 5.9–turn left on Buck Forest Rd and cross through covered bridge. Just the other side of the bridge, turn right on Pipeline Trail.
- Mile 6.3–turn right on High Falls Trail and ride down to the shelter to view the falls. Turn around at the shelter and head back up High Falls Trail, then turn right on Triple Falls Trail.
- Mile 7.5–High Falls Trail exits right.
- Mile 7.6–turn left on Galax Tr.
- Mile 8.0–turn right on Staton Rd, and cross bridge to finish.

Joanna Mtn

Jct Buck Forest Rd

3000'

2000'

Bridal Veil Falls has to be on your *"don't miss it"* list for Dupont. Getting there this way requires a wet river crossing, but until the right-of-way dispute with AGFA is settled, it's the best way. This map also shows other trails to use, if and when there is a right-of-way across AGFA property.

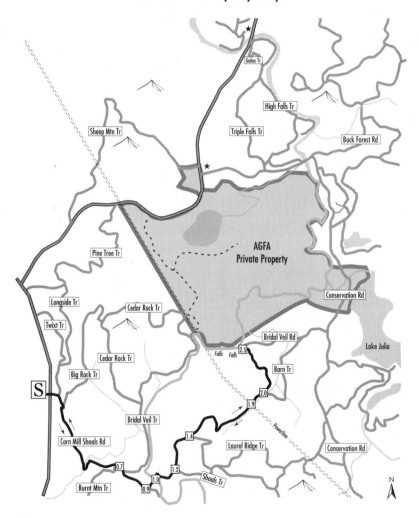

START/FINISH
Cascade Lake Road
Trailhead Parking

TRAIL CONFIGURATION
Out-and-Back

SURFACE
Double track • 5 miles

HIGHLIGHTS
Sandy road, slippery &
wet river crossing,
spectcular falls, bare
rock riding

TOTAL DISTANCE
5 miles

TIME ALLOWANCE
(Includes hanging
out at the falls)
Beginner • 3 hours
Intermediate • 2.5 hours
Advanced • 2 hours

Mileposts

- From start–ride across road and onto Corn Mill Shoals Road. You'll take this road/trail all the way to the falls. A number of trails enter along the way, but I'll only highlight where it's not obvious which way to go.
- Mile 0.7–Bridal Veil Trail exits to the left. Stay on Corn Mill Shoals Rd.
- Mile 0.9–Little River Trail exits to the right. Stay on C M Shoals Rd.
- Mile 1.0–cross Little River at Corn Mill Shoals. Take care; it's slippery
- Mile 1.2–Shoals Trail exits right
- Mile 1.4–Laurel Ridge Tr exits right
- Mile 1.9–cross under powerline
- Mile 2.0–turn left to stay on Corn Mill Shoals Rd/Trail. Barn Trail continues straight ahead.
- Mile 2.5–base of Bridal Veil Falls. There's plenty to explore here before heading back the way you came in.
- Mile 5.0–finish.

Corn Mill Shoals   Bridal Veil Falls   Corn Mill Shoals

2000'

Flatwoods Easy

*T*he most level terrain in Dupont State Forest is in (where else?) the Flatwoods area. Still, there's not much of it. This short route takes advantage of the scarce flats and makes a good ride for those just getting started on mountain bikes.

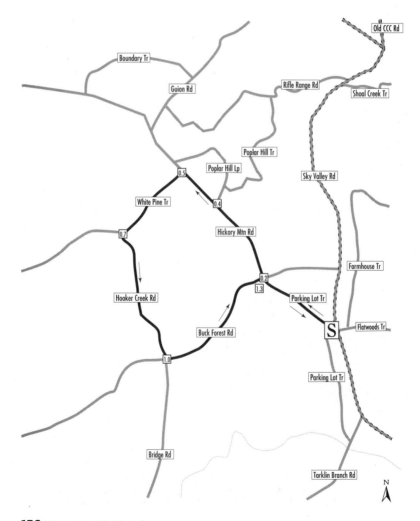

START/FINISH
Flatwoods Trailhead Parking on Sky Valley Road

TRAIL CONFIGURATION
Loop

SURFACE
Double track • 1.5 miles

HIGHLIGHTS
No hills, wide trails, some loose rocks, a few sandy spots, horse use

TOTAL DISTANCE
1.5 miles

TIME ALLOWANCE
Beginner • 45 min
Intermediate • 20 min
Advanced • 15 min

Mileposts

- From start–ride out of parking lot and across field above house and shelter.
- Mile 0.2–continue straight across Buck Forest Road onto Hickory Mountain Road.
- Mile 0.4–Poplar Hill Loop exits on the right. Stay straight on Hickory Mountain Road.
- Mile 0.5–turn left on White Pine Trail.
- Mile 0.7–bear left on Hooker Creek Road.
- Mile 1.0–turn left on Buck Forest Road.
- Mile 1.3–turn right back towards trailhead parking area.
- Mile 1.5–finish.

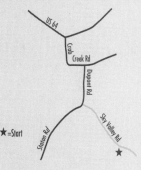

US 64

Crab Creek Rd

Dupont Rd

Sky Valley Rd

Staton Rd

★ =Start

★

2000'

1000'

Flatwoods Moderate

This route is the next step up in difficulty when it comes to riding in the Flatwoods. It's longer, there are some technical sections, and there are some hills to climb. You get to go down a few, too, and they're a real hoot.

Mileposts

- From start–cross road onto Flatwoods Trail.
- Mile 0.2–turn left on Shoal Creek Trail.
- Mile 0.6–Farmhouse Trail exits left.
- Mile 1–cross roadway onto Rifle Range Rd (it's a trail!).
- Mile 1.2–Poplar Hill Tr exits left.
- Mile 1.5–turn left on Guion Rd.
- Mile 1.6–turn right on Hickory Mountain Road.
- Mile 1.8–Boudary Trail exits right.
- Mile 2.1–turn left on Range Loop.
- Mile 2.4–turn left on Hooker Creek Road.
- Mile 3.5–turn right on White Pine Tr.
- Mile 3.8–cross Buck Forest Road onto Bridge Road.
- Mile 4.6–turn left on Tarklin Branch Road.
- Mile 5.0–bear left to stay on Tarklin Branch Road.
- Mile 5.1–left to stay on Tarklin Br.
- Mile 6–bear left.
- Mile 6.2–finish.

START/FINISH
Flatwoods Trailhead Parking on Sky Valley Road

TRAIL CONFIGURATION
Loop

SURFACE
Double/Single track • 6.2 miles

HIGHLIGHTS
Horse use, small stream crossings, rocky sections, sandy sections, washout areas, whoops, short steep climbs

TOTAL DISTANCE
6.2 miles

TIME ALLOWANCE
Beginner • 2 hours
Intermediate • 1.5 hours
Advanced • 1 hour

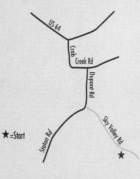

 =Start

Rifle Range Rd   Hooker Cr Rd   Tarklin Branch

2000'

1000'

Flatwoods Difficult

his ride takes in the all the best the Flatwoods has to offer. Short but tough climbs, whoops on the downhills, a waterfall, smooth single track, and a sprinkling of technical sections. There's an old cemetery to explore and in winter you can soak in some pretty good views. Beware of the sand and look out for horses.

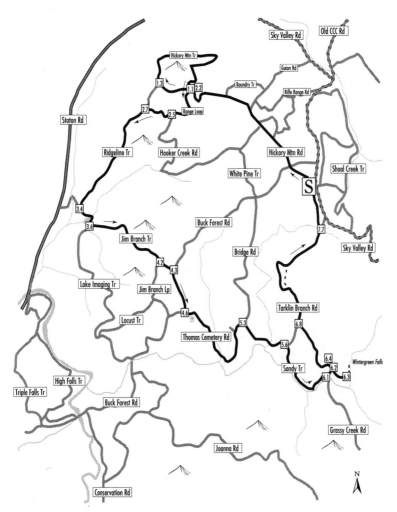

START/FINISH
Flatwoods Trailhead Parking on Sky Valley Road

TRAIL CONFIGURATION
Loop

SURFACE
Single/Double track • 7.9 miles

HIGHLIGHTS
winter views, technical sections, horse use, sand, whoop-te-doos, small stream crossings, Wintergreen Falls

TOTAL DISTANCE
7.9 miles

TIME ALLOWANCE
Beginner • 3 hours
Intermediate • 2+ hours
Advanced • 1.5 hours

Mileposts

- From start–ride out back of parking area through field behind houses and onto Hickory Mtn Rd. Stay on it as trails and roads exit
- Mile 1.1–turn left on Hickory Mountain Trail. Do not yet take Range Loop, which is a hard left.
- Mile 1.3–bear right to remain on Hickory Mountain Trail.
- Mile 2.2–turn right, this time on Range Loop.
- Mile 2.5–Hooker Creek Road exits left. Stay on Range Loop.
- Mile 2.7–turn left on Ridgeline Tr.
- Mile 3.4–left on Lake Imaging Tr.
- Mile 3.6–turn left on Jim Branch Tr.
- Mile 4.2–Continue straight. Jim Branch Loop exits right.
- Mile 4.3–right on Buck Forest Rd.
- Mile 4.6–left on Thomas Cemetery Road.
- Mile 5.3–right on Tarklin Br Rd.
- Mile 5.6–turn right on Sandy Trail.
- Mile 6.1–turn left on Grassy Creek Road. Do not cross creek.
- Mile 6.2–turn right on Wintergreen Falls Trail.
- Mile 6.3–view falls then turn back.
- Mile 6.4–turn right on Grassy Creek Road.
- Mile 6.8–continue straight onto Tarklin Branch Road.
- Mile 7.9–finish.

Hickory Mtn

Lake Imaging

Wintergreen Falls

2000'

1000'

Grassy-Briery

A *difficult ride that takes in a portion of the Flatwoods, then heads off to explore the more remote sections of Grassy and then Briery Creek. You'll find it a mixture of sandy, rocky trails and smooth forest trails. There are stream crossings, technical climbs and at least one real teeth-rattling descent.*

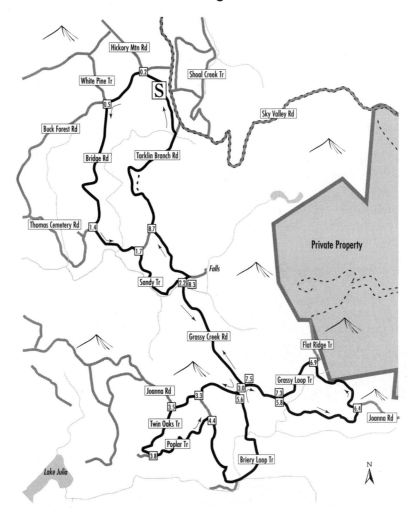

START/FINISH
Flatwoods Trailhead
Parking on Sky Valley
Road

TRAIL CONFIGURATION
Double lollipop loop

SURFACE
Single/Double track •
9.8 miles

HIGHLIGHTS
rocks, roots, stream
crossings, sand, horse
use, waterfall, winter
views, whoops

TOTAL DISTANCE
9.8 miles

TIME ALLOWANCE
Beginner • not advised
Intermediate • 2+ hours
Advanced • 1.5 hours

Mileposts

- From start–ride out across field behind houses.
- Mile 0.2–left on Buck Forest Road.
- Mile 0.5–turn left on Bridge Road.
- Mile 1.4–turn left on Tarklin Road.
- Mile 1.7–turn right on Sandy Trail.
- Mile 2.2–turn right and cross creek on Grassy Creek Road.
- Mile 3.0–turn right on Joanna Road. Stay on it until Twin Oaks.
- Mile 3.5–turn left on Twin Oaks Tr.
- Mile 3.8–turn left on Poplar Trail.
- Mile 4.4–right on Briery Loop Trail.
- Mile 5.3–turn right on Joanna Rd.
- Mile 5.8–Grassy Loop Trail enters from left. Stay on Joanna Road.
- Mile 6.4–turn left on Grassy LoopTr.
- Mile 6.9–at wildlife field turn left on far side to stay on Grassy LpTr.
- Mile 7.3–turn right on Joanna Rd.
- Mile 7.5–right on Grassy Creek Rd.
- Mile 8.3–cross creek and turn right to remain on Grassy Creek Rd.
- Mile 8.7–straight onto Tarklin Br Rd.
- Mile 9.8–finish.

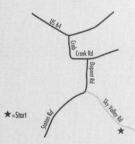

★ =Start

US 64
Crab Creek Rd
Dupont Rd
Seton Rd
Sky Valley Rd

Grassy Creek

Briery Creek

Grassy Loop Tr

2000'
1000'

Casual Dupont

*W*ant to see some of the major features of Dupont, but don't want to work too hard? Here's your ride. You'll see several large waterfalls, the covered bridge, pavillions, and other sights. If and when the right-of-way is settled with AGFA, you can head on over to Lake Julia and Bridal Veil Falls without much trouble.

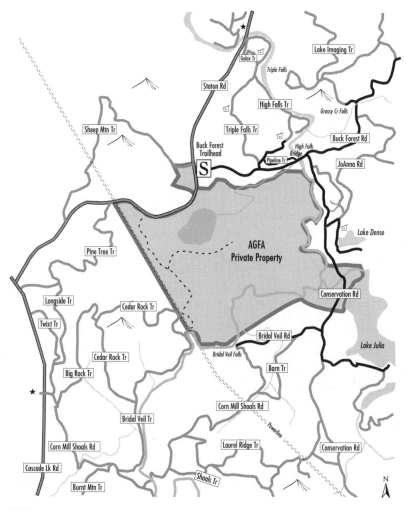

Lake Imaging Tr

Galax Tr

Triple Falls

Staton Rd

High Falls Tr

Grassy Cr Falls

Sheep Mtn Tr

Triple Falls Tr

Buck Forest Rd

Buck Forest Trailhead

S

High Falls Bridge

Pipeline Tr

JoAnna Rd

Lake Dense

Pine Tree Tr

AGFA Private Property

Longside Tr

Cedar Rock Tr

Conservation Rd

Twixt Tr

Bridal Veil Rd

Cedar Rock Tr

Bridal Veil Falls

Lake Julia

Big Rock Tr

Barn Tr

Corn Mill Shoals Rd

Bridal Veil Tr

Corn Mill Shoals Rd

Laurel Ridge Tr

Conservation Rd

Cascade Lk Rd

Powerline

Burnt Mtn Tr

Shoals Tr

N

START/FINISH
Buck Forest Trailhead
on Staton Road

TRAIL CONFIGURATION
Out-and-Back

SURFACE
Forest road

HIGHLIGHTS
Few hills, loose gravel,
waterfall views, lake
view, covered bridge,
picnic pavillions

TOTAL DISTANCE
1-8 miles

TIME ALLOWANCE
Take as much time on
this one as you like and
explore around. It's not
meant to be a sprint.

Mileposts

- It's 0.6 miles from the trailhead to the covered bridge at the top of High Falls.
- If you want to ride out to get a look at High Falls from across the way at the picnic shelter, it's 0.3 miles from the bridge via Pipeline and then High Falls Trail.
- If you want to go and look at Triple Falls it requires a more difficult ride (downhill going out, uphill return) via Triple Falls Trail. Its 1.4 miles from Buck Forest Road to the viewing shelter.
- If you want to view Grassy Creek Falls, take Buck Forest Road to Lake Imaging Trail (it's a road, too). You'll have to climb a bit to get there and then hike down to view the falls. It's 0.8 miles from the covered bridge.
- Should the right-of-way be open across the AGFA property, you can go see Lake Julia and Bridal Veil Falls. It's 1.8 miles to Lake Julia from the bridge and 1.6 miles to Bridal Veil Falls from the bridge.

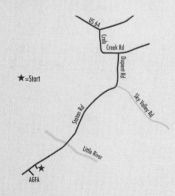

Appendix

Local Bike Resources

ASHEVILLE AREA

• Liberty Bicycles
1378 Hendersonville Hwy.
Asheville, NC 28803
828-684-1085
www.LibertyBikes.com
Sales, rentals and repairs
services

• Pro Bikes of Asheville
793 Merrimon Ave.
Asheville, NC 28804
828-253-2800
Sales and repair services

• Carolina Fatz
Mountain Bike Center
1240 Brevard Road #3
Asheville, NC 28806
828-665-8009
Sales, rentals and repair
services   *Downhill Stuff*
On The way to BentCreek.

• Hearn's Cycling
34 Broadway
Asheville, NC 28801
828-253-4800
www.hearnscycling.com
Sales and repair services.

• Ski Country Sports
960 Merrimon Ave
Asheville, NC 28804
828-254-2771
www.skicountrysports.com
Sales, service, rentals and
guided rides

• Black Bear Adventures
215 Oak Terrace Rd
Asheville, NC 28806
828-670-7174
Guide and tour services

• Bio Wheels
76 Biltmore Ave
Asheville, NC 28801
828-232-0300
www.biowheels.com
Sales, rentals, tours and repair
services

• Cane Creek Cycling
Components
335 Cane Creek Rd
Fletcher, NC 38732
828-684-3551
www.canecreek.com
Manufactures cycling components; big supporter of
Asheville bicycling

• Breakaway Bicycle Shop
230 Rutledge Rd #26
Fletcher, NC 28732
828-775-3730
Sales and repair services

PISGAH FOREST

- **Backcountry Outdoors**
  Corner of 276 & 64
  18 Pisgah Hwy.
  Pisgah Forest, NC 28768
  828-884-4262
  www.backcountryoutdoors.com
  Sales, rentals and repair
  services

BREVARD

- **Sycamore Cycles**
  118 W Main St
  Brevard, NC 28712
  828-877-5790
  Sales and repair services

HENDERSONVILLE

- **Bikeways**
  607 Greenville Hwy.
  Hendersonville, NC 28739
  828-692-0613
  Sales and repair services

- **The Bicycle Company of Hendersonville**
  779-A N Church St
  Hendersonville, NC 28739
  Sales and repair services

ADVOCACY GROUPS

- **Blue Ridge Bicycle Club**
  PO Box 309
  Asheville, NC 28802
  www.blueridgebicycleclub.org

- **Friends of Dupont State Forest**
  PO Box 42
  Hendersonville, NC 28793
  trailboss@dupontforest.com
  www.dupontforest.com

Lodging & Camping

Lodging establishments abound in the area surrounding both the Pisgah National Forest and the Dupont State Forest. Depending on which area you choose to ride, you might stay in or near Asheville, somewhere around Brevard or Pisgah Forest, or nearer Hendersonville. The choices run the gamut from fancy lodge and B & B accommodations to quaint road-side motels. Listed below are the chambers of commerce for the different areas. These organizations can give you the most up-to-date information on what is available and help you out if you have specific needs. I've also listed a few places that are a little out of the ordinary or have in the past specifically catered to mountain bikers. Whatever you choose, be sure to call ahead for reservations, especially in the busy seasons from mid-June through August and during in the month of October.

LOCAL CHAMBERS

- **Brevard Chamber of Commerce**
  35 W. Main Street
  Brevard, NC 28712
  800-648-4523
  www.brevardncchamber.org

- **Asheville Area Chamber of Commerce**
  PO Box 1010
  Asheville, NC 28801
  800-257-1300
  www.ashevillechamber.org

- **Hendersonville Area Chamber of Commerce**
  330 N King St
  Hendersonville, NC 28792
  828-692-1413
  www.hendersonvillechamber.org

NATIONAL FOREST CAMPGROUNDS

In the Pisgah District, free roadside camping is permitted in areas so designated by a sign. Camping is also permitted any-where in the backcountry if you are at least 500 feet from an open road. There are also three very nice public campgrounds and two groups-only campgrounds. Contact the ranger office if you've got a large group; the rates are very reasonable.

PUBLIC CAMPGROUNDS

- **Davidson River Campground**
  First-come, first-served; designated sites; per-site fee; hot showers; closed in winter

- **North Mills River Campground**
  First-come, first-served; designated sites; per-site fee; hot showers; closed in winter

- **Lake Powhatan Campground**
  First-come, first-served; designated sites; per-site fee; hot showers; closed in winter

GROUP CAMPGROUNDS

- **Cove Creek Group Camp**
  Reservations required, groups only, primitive facilities

- **White Pines Group Camp**
  Reservations required, groups only, primitive facilities

For more information contact:
Pisgah Ranger District
1001 Pisgah Hwy.
Pisgah Forest, NC 28768
828-877-3265

DUPONT STATE FOREST

Currently, camping is not permitted in Dupont State Forest. Davidson River Campground in Pisgah National Forest is about 25 minutes away. Also, a private campground is located on US 276 in Cedar Mountain.

- **Black Forest Family Camping Resort**
  PO Box 709
  Summer Rd/US 276
  Cedar Mountain, NC 28718
  828-884-2267
  www.blackforestcampground.com

SELECTED LODGING

- **Key Falls Inn**
  151 Everett Road
  Pisgah Forest, NC 28768
  828-884-7559 or
  toll free 877-684-6833
  www.bbdirectory.com/Inn/Key-falls-inn
  Bed & Breakfast, away from town, close to most trails

- **Trails End**
  Operated by Liberty Bicycles
  1387 Hendersonville Hwy.
  Asheville, NC 28803
  828-684-1085
  www.LibertyBikes.com
  On the very edge of Bent Creek Forest

- **The Pisgah Inn**
  P.O. Drawer 749
  Waynesville, NC 28786
  828-235-8228
  Located on the Blue Ridge Parkway, great views, restaurant
  Open April – November

Notes

6-21-00 Turkey Pen TH. S. Mills River Trail to
Cantrell Creek Trail (muddy, Loose Rock, roots,
overgrown vegitation, Horror fest) Ⓡ on
Squirel Gap Trail, Ⓑ on Mullinax Trail.
Back to Turkey Pen TH.

Mullinax : Good Tech Trail ē many waterbars. R 4
Squirel Gap: Tight, Slow, Tech, Sidehill, Singletrach R 2.5
Cantrell Creek: Sucks, Stay Away. R .5

6-28-00 Combined Clawhammer ē Buckhorn Gap.
went counterclockwise, Pushed to top of Clawhammer.
Then pushed Down other side due to Steps &
Switchbacks. Easier to go South on Black MTN
Trail. Took BMT to Avery Creek Trail back to
Stable. Lots of trees down on Avery Creek Trail
Clawhammer very tech. Avery Tech DH.   ≈ 12 miles

10-19-02 Cedar Rock

Did most of the Loop Backwards, Slickrock areas
are Easy. Burnt MTN Tr is an awsome downhill after
Topping the MTN. Lots of tight, wooded Singletrach with
Lots of jumps and a steep or two.

10-23-02 OID Sidehill

A maze with very few trail markings. Easy to
get Lost.

10-24-02 Perry Cove

Rode in Rain. Very Slick, but fun. The ride up the
road sucks! The Singletrack is Awsome. Starts
as a ridge ride then starts going down. Good Tech
rocks/roots on Bennett Gap. Perry Cove easyer but fun,
was told Bennett Gap is cool also.

Notes

10-21-02 Kitsuma

East on I40 exit 66. Go ⓛ over interstate and turn ⓡ.
Pass Ridgecrest to stop sign. Go Strait to Parking Lot
at End of Street. Trail Starts on E side of P Lot.
AT End of trail, Exit Picnic area going ⓛ up
dead end road. This is Old Hwy 70. follow 4-5
miles back to Parking Lot. Trail has multiple Switchbacks
going up, one Steep Saddle, Fast tight ridge run,
Super fun.

≅ 10 miles RT
≅ 2 hrs

5-11-12 Jackrabbit Trails

Hwy 64 west from Franklin. Turn South (ⓛ) on
Hwy 175. TH next to Phyladelphia Church.
We did ride Counter Clockwise. Rode all the trails
High Point trail best S to N. Fast, Flowy Singletrach.
Non Technical. Scenic. Plenty of swimming in
Summer. SABt Beach very cool.

Notes

5-24-12   Bent Creek Area.

Parked at 479E. Took FR 479E up to
Ingles Field Gap Trail. Then up N. Boundry
Rd (AKA FR 485). Wide easy Double & Single track.
Was starting to think it was Lame until we
took Green's Lick down. Looked for
mo Heinous & Betty heinous but couldn't
find them. After Green Lick Trail Junction,
The trail (485) became overgrown and unused.
Green Lick is sick!!! Wall rides at top.
Banked Turns and big jumps down Low.
Reminded me of a rough, natural "Rainmaker"
worth the ride up. Do this Ride!

Notes

Milestone Press
Outdoor Adventure Guides

MOUNTAIN BIKE SERIES

OFF THE BEATEN TRACK
by Jim Parham
• *Vol. I: WNC—The Smokies*
• *Vol. II: WNC—Pisgah*
• *Vol. III: North Georgia*
• *Vol. IV: East Tennessee*
• *Vol. V: Northern Virginia*
• *Vol. VI: WV—Northern Highlands*

• *Tsali Mountain Bike Trails Map*
• *Bull Mountain Bike Trails Map*

ROAD BIKE SERIES

• *Road Bike Asheville, NC: Favorite Rides of the Blue Ridge Bicycle Club* by The Blue Ridge Bicycle Club

• *Road Bike the Smokies: 16 Great Rides in North Carolina's Great Smoky Mountains* by Jim Parham

• *Road Bike North Georgia: 25 Great Rides in the Mountains and Valleys of North Georgia* by Jim Parham

PLAYBOATING

• *A Playboater's Guide to the Ocoee River*
• *Playboating the Nantahala River— An Entry Level Guide* by Kelly Fischer

FAMILY ADVENTURE SERIES

• *Natural Adventures in the Mountains of Western NC*
• *Natural Adventures in the Mountains of North Georgia* by Mary Ellen Hammond & Jim Parham

MOTORCYCLE SERIES

• *Motorcycle Adventures in the Southern Appalachian— North GA, East TN, Western NC*
• *Motorcycle Adventures in the Southern Appalachians— Asheville NC, Blue Ridge Parkway, NC High Country* by Hawk Hagebak

A NOTE TO THE READER

Can't find the Milestone Press book you want at a bookseller, bike shop or outfitter store near you? Don't despair—you can order it directly from us. Write: Milestone Press, PO Box 158, Almond, NC 28702; call us at 828-488-6601; or dial us up and shop on line at www.milestonepress.com.

We welcome your comments and suggestions regarding the contents of this book. Please write us at the address above or e-mail us at: otbt2@milestonepress.com.